P9-BJO-724

EXPERIMENT AT EVERGREEN

EXPERIMENT AT EVERGREEN

By
Richard M. Jones

LIBRARY-MEDIA CENTER
SOUTH PUGET SOUND COMM. COLLEGE
2011 MOTTMAN RD. S.W.
OLYMPIA, WA 98512-6292

Schenkman Publishing Company, Inc.

Cambridge, Massachusetts

WITHDRAWN

Copyright © 1981
Schenkman Publishing Company Inc.
3 Mount Auburn Place
Cambridge, Massachusetts 02138

Library of Congress Cataloging in Publication Data
Jones, Richard Matthew, 1925–
    Experiment at Evergreen.

    1. Evergreen State College – History. 2. Education,
Humanistic. I. Title.
LD1761.E68J66   378.797'79   81–391
ISBN 0-87073-838-0   AACR1
ISBN 0-87073-839-9 (pbk)

Printed in the United States of America

All rights reserved. This book, or parts thereof, may not be reproduced
in any form without permission from the publisher.

041932

CONTENTS

I dedicate this report to
Mervyn Cadwallader
and
Charles McCann
without whose vision and support
the experience on which the report is based
would not have been possible.

What we need to consider
is not an addition to our teaching procedure,
but a transformation of it.

Alexander Meiklejohn, 1931

PREFACE

The student unrest of the 1960s, and the demands it made for improvements in the quality of undergraduate teaching, resulted in a number of state-instituted "alternative" colleges. Wisconsin offered its alternative at Green Bay; Texas offered its alternative at Permian Basin; California offered its alternative at Santa Cruz; Maryland offered its alternative at St. Mary's State College; Michigan offered its alternative at Thomas Jefferson College; New Jersey offered its alternatives at Ramapo and Stockton; New York offered its alternatives at Empire State and Old Westbury.

All of these attempts to explore new ways of serving the educational needs of America's young people have stirred controversy. All have had to contend with opposition from vested interests in the traditional ways of serving these needs, and all have had to make compromises with that opposition. Not all have survived as alternative colleges, and those which have survived have maintained their integrity as experiments in varying degrees. The state of Washington's offering, The Evergreen State College, has been one of the most definite in its commitment to a distinctive alternative, and it has both survived and maintained its conceptual integrity for a surprising length of time.

The following is not a report on The Evergreen State College as such. It is a report on the particular innovation in which the college has invested most of its resources and for which it is best known: programs of coordinated study.

Ideally, the reader of this report should have first read *The Experimental College,* by Alexander Meiklejohn (Arno Press, 1932); and *Experiment at Berkeley,* by Joseph Tussman (Oxford University Press, 1969), as these books provide the history of the coordinated studies concept prior to its becoming the central mission of The Evergreen State College. Neither book is now widely available, however; and, in any event, the Evergreen experience has been so much longer and so much more diversified that its previous versions can only be of historical significance. Nevertheless, those who may read this report with enthusiasm will want to locate library copies of Meiklejohn's and Tussman's books, as the three reports, taken in sequence, chart the evolution of a fascinating cultural gene in its possible recessive phases.

I wish to emphasize that the report is an *individual* one. In writing it I sought to reflect on my own experiences, and on my observations of the experiences of colleagues and students, as accurately as possible. Therefore, I, alone, am responsible for whatever inaccurate perceptions or biased conclusions the report may include.

— Richard M. Jones

INTRODUCTION

What is the undergraduate education for? What ought to be taught? How should it be taught? If we can get anywhere with the first of the questions, the other two ought to be somewhat easier, at least, to think about.

The heart of the matter is the liberal arts. For better or worse, most other curricular questions are being answered today by the known (or "projected") demands to be placed on graduates in the "real world" for which their educations are supposedly preparing them. While it is true that many people object to forced solutions based on cash-value pragmatism in our colleges and universities, those objections can mean little in the present and projected economic climate. Even as the professors and deans argue among themselves, they are being told the answers — from outside and from above. (The degree of bluntness with which the answers get told to them is mostly a matter of individual institutions' enrollment problems and retention problems.) The main thing left up to internal professorial argument is the liberal arts. The amount of professorial "say so" there is, I think, dwindling too. The cash-value

stuff is slowly crowding the liberal arts out, and in many institutions the condition already prevails of not having much left
to argue about at all.

Yet the argument must go on. For the irony is that the liberal
arts are crucial to all institutions which call themselves colleges
or universities and which purport to offer undergraduate
degrees. The crucialness I speak of is not merely a matter of my
idealism in calling it such, or of their idealism in thinking of
it as such. It is also a matter of practicality; a large question of
individual and collective institutional identity is at stake. The
institutions know full well that they cannot continue to call
themselves colleges and universities if they continue to allow
— or to force — the shrinkage of the liberal arts curriculum. The
ultimate irony would be an ivy-covered little college somewhere
in Vermont which, pressed for cash and for the warm bodies
which pay it in tuition, simply stopped offering the liberal arts
altogether. (It has doubtless already happened — somewhere.)
But the vast majority of our institutions is by no means ready
to give up on the liberal arts and to concentrate solely on
preprofessional, paraprofessional, and vocational training. Even
if their administrative officers, fighting insomnia late into the
night, might sometimes wish that they could go in the next
day and axe the liberal arts, they know that they cannot. For
who — and what — would they be, if they did?

As it happens, there is only the one common denominator
in higher education: the liberal arts. Only this fact, I think,
will save them in the hundreds of institutions which now lack
either the prestige or the money to get and to retain enough
students. (And it must be remembered that many of these
beleagured institutions are excellent ones, and that all of
them, taken together, are the majority.) For colleges and
universities have traditionally been defined, and have defined
themselves, as places which offered — either exclusively or in
the center of everything else — "an excellent education in the
liberal arts." (That not all such education has been excellent
is neither here nor there; I am speaking of the ways in which
the institutions have thought of themselves and advertised
themselves to the world.)

Only in comparatively recent times have these institutions
undertaken to train graduate students (in much of anything

other than theology, medicine, and law), to prepare their under-graduates specifically for graduate school rigors, and to take on the task of educating undergraduates for particular para-professional and vocational jobs. In very recent times, however, these kinds of institutional sidelines have been moving toward the center of the store. Moreover, they have been joined by an ever-expanding group of yet newer sidelines: cooperative education (usually in the form of work-study internships for academic credit); so-called "outreach" programs; lower-division credit for "life experience," and so on.

As any institution's funds are finite, and as funders are understandably reluctant to pour their dollars into the insti-tutions as unquestioningly as they once could and did, the sidelines are more and more chipping away at the liberal arts' territory — merely through winning budgetary battles. Yet, for the reason I gave above, they cannot win *the* battle: the liberal arts will survive, *if only because* the people who run the colleges and universities must continue, at the very least, to pay lip-service to them. I must note here that I feel very sorry for those administrators caught, in the majority of American institutions of higher learning, in the past two decades and the one just beginning. The accompanying cartoon from *The New Yorker* shows what is going on around many administrative

"We've got to give the appearance of changing direction without giving the appearance of changing principles in a way that won't be dismissed as cosmetic."

tables today. I have sat briefly at such tables, and they are insufferable places to be sitting – at any wage. Most administrators, to their credit, know this. Those who don't know it are terrifying.

At the very least, then, we are going to continue having something called the liberal arts in most institutions. That much is solid. The only questions are: how much? and how good? Today, the answer to the latter will be the answer to the former, as the liberal arts are, like it or not, competing. The rest of this introduction will be given over to some talk about the realities of that competition and to one strategy for competing well – the one which this book is about.

II

For the first question raised above – what is the undergraduate curriculum for? – we can now substitute another: what is the liberal arts curriculum for? (I repeat that all the other questions will be answered for us – or most of them, anyway – while the liberal arts question remains very much unanswered.) For all of its difficulties, this is at least a narrower question; and because of the inarguable centrality of the liberal arts, it is a more interesting one.

There are only two possible answers. One is new, and one is old. The new one runs as follows: "The liberal arts curriculum, since we have to have it, is for attracting the largest possible number of students into our liberal arts program, in order that we can all keep our jobs and maybe even hire a lot more analogues to ourselves. Then, maybe we can begin to regain some lost territory and some lost power around this place. Therefore, the liberal arts curriculum ought to be something which we can *call* liberal arts – while filling it full of what your average 17-year-old or your average retiree in America can be expected to want." (This approach leads to courses in "futurology," 1940s movies, sociological studies of comic books; and to such texts as *The Greening of America, The Tao of Physics,* and *When Worlds Collide.* In a more general way, it leads to curricula which mirror whatever intellectual fad is in the saddle; for the last ten years, it has been third- [and fourth- and fifth-

and sixth-] force psychology, a hydra-headed monster which is only now retreating, and which will only die when it is finally laughed to death by a generation lacking the peculiar combination of affluence and ignorance which spawned it.)

The older answer is this: the liberal arts curriculum should prepare people to live both an interesting life of the mind and a committed life of active citizenship in the fifty-odd years following college graduation. (These two lives are not necessarily mutually exclusive; but they can be expected to be independent of each other with many individuals.) It should, moreover, prepare people to be committed participants in both arenas through speaking and writing. For those who do not seek schooling beyond the bachelor's degree, this preparation will make life more interesting for both the unemployed and the drudgingly employed over the long haul. It will also enable them to be more effective in whatever roles they choose to play in making a better world between now and 2030. (I am assuming here, perhaps too cynically, that most of these roles will be played *outside* the job role, if there is a job role at all; if this be cynicism, it is based on my perceptions of people's job experiences, based in turn on what people tell me about their jobs.) Those who go on for further schooling (and for the degrees which terminate it) may likewise be either unemployed or drudgingly employed; but their odds — in terms of overall statistics — are better. That is, they have a better chance of linking up the life of the mind and the life of citizenship with a professional role of some kind. It follows, therefore, that such preparation should be made up of "the best that has been thought and said" — except that to that Victorian formulation should be added the best possible grounding in the natural sciences. (Such a grounding is too often left out — even today.)

Here, we begin to see some daylight in our long night of the soul with these difficult questions, because . . . *we know what the books are.* The only problem is that of what to leave out, as there are far too many ancient and modern classics, and far too much science, to teach in four years. So we do, then, know what to teach; and it is only a question of being brave enough — good enough — to start teaching it.

III

Before going further, I'd like to answer some objections which I've anticipated to the foregoing.

First, isn't it elitist to suggest that we teach such a curriculum? I don't think so. As I said, I think that most liberal arts professors are themselves agreed as to what the best books are and as to what an excellent undergraduate training in the natural sciences would be like, and can argue only about what would have to go, given four·years. Therefore, *not* to teach those books, and *not* to give that training, would be more in accord with our historical understanding of elitist power. In a wonderful book called *Less Than Words Can Say*, Professor Richard Mitchell states this case better than most people have ever managed:

> [The poor and uneducated] are a reactionary's dream, an utterly stable segment of society. Every year, without fail, they will consume just so much junk, just so many TV dinners, and just so many pay-by-the-week burial-expense insurance policies. They will invest a predictable proportion of what little they have in lottery tickets and patent medicines. They will keep the whole legal system employed by committing, quite regularly, an ever-growing number of crimes, mostly against each other, fortunately. Some few of them will always provide a never-failing pool of utterly unskilled labor to do the necessary scut-work that underlies the technology that the rest of us can handle. They will support prodigiously the enormous illegal drug industry and contribute vast sums to all those along the line who profit from it. . . . They will buy couches and lamps and refrigerators of the sleaziest quality on the never-never plan at fantastic rates of interest. There is simply no counting the benefits they bestow on the rest of us. . . .
>
> A person who speaks and writes his native tongue clearly and precisely does so because of many other abilities, and those abilities themselves grow stronger through the fluent manipulation of language. The simple matter of being logical is a function of language. A million high school graduates capable of fluent English would be a million Americans capable of logical thought. What would we do with them. . . ? You think *they're* going to buy those lottery tickets and lamps in the shape of Porky Pig? You think they're going to

hang out on the corners and provide employment for everybody from the local social worker to the justices of the Supreme Court? Well, don't worry. It's just a bad dream. . . .

When we look around the country and see that school-children are more ignorant than ever. . . , we are inclined to think that something has failed. That is a naive conclusion. In fact, something has succeeded.

(Mitchell is referring mainly to the black, urban poor in the passage, and he is talking specifically of the issues of teaching them standard English in the schools. But we are making the same reply to the charge of "elitism," as I think Mitchell would agree.)

Second, some would say that the advocacy of a "great books" curriculum and of a strong science curriculum is actually a cry to return to the "good old days," back when there were "standards." But the truth is that those "good old days" in higher education were a time of far fewer students – and far fewer institutions – than we have now. It is true that curricula such as I advocate have been offered before, but they were offered only to a very few people – mostly the wealthy and the highly talented. And those few people were almost all men who were between the ages of 17 and 22. Since the end of World War II, very few institutions have done much by way of offering the above as "mass education," and very few have done much to "popularize" such an education to the masses.

I do not believe that the masses have been as complicitous in the backing-away from great education as the institutions like to believe. In any event, the idea of the *isolated course* as the basic element in the curricular structure has militated against great education in most places, no matter what was being taught. That idea has greatly outlived its usefulness – except for basic, skills-building work, for which it will probably always be necessary. It is time now for us to teach the liberal arts as they ought to be taught: in interdisciplinary programs staffed by good teachers who are excellent in at least one specialty area but proficient in several. This has almost never been done in a serious way, that is, as a serious institutional commitment. The "good old days" were filled with (mostly unmemorable) courses, as the reader will remember.

Third, it is often argued that a "great books" curriculum is an impractical luxury for those students who must go out and try to find a job after graduation. All idealistic talk aside (talk about how such an education is good for such students, and good for their country and their world), I believe that the argument of impracticality is largely an idle one today. An increasing number of certification programs which terminate with associate or baccalaureate degrees simply do not guarantee the jobs which they were meant to assure. (Teacher certification is perhaps the most dramatic case in point.) At the community college level, the certification situation is especially instructive. Although most citizens are not yet aware of it, our vast community college network is in some trouble. The reasons have to do with the rationale for its founding, in the first place, back in the 1960s. And, again, most people don't know much about the circumstances of that founding.

A recent poll showed that Americans know little about what community colleges were set up to do. Most surveyed citizens thought that such colleges are primarily preparatory schools in the liberal arts. But the truth is that they specialize in paraprofessional job-readiness certification. In the early 1960s, the experts thought that such certification was a good thing to provide for, not only because it might be intrinsically valuable, and not only because it might be a good alternative to "real" college for some young people, but also – and mostly – because of widespread certitude that the jobs would be there for the AAs. Now, it is clear that the jobs will *not* be there; and this fact is as clear to the prospective students as it is to the professional worriers. (In my own state, a recent study prepared for the legislature foresees that about half of the community colleges will need to be closed down in the 1980s, and contingency plans are already in the works for the conversion of their campuses into other badly needed facilities.)

The truth is simply that AA and BA certification programs increasingly fail to certify in any way other than granting a *certificate* – a piece of paper. Such paper is now increasingly unrelated to real markets.

I have so far mentioned only the impact on stud
dangerous lack of relatedness between pieces of paper and
markets. What of the impact on institutions?

Well, if enough students decide that their certification will
be unrelated to their job hopes, and if they therefore decide
to drop out (or not to attend in the first place), and if the price
of a college education keeps going up (in 1979–80, we saw a
10 percent increase in tuition costs), then some of the colleges
and universities stand the chance of taking a great fall. Their
overinvestment (and consequent overextension) in certification
programs is serious at present, and the collapse of the house
of cards which is now in place would mean the loss of countless
professorial and staff jobs. The institutions would of course
survive such a collapse – most of them, anyway – but reorgani-
zation would be torturous and anomie-producing for them.
Moreover, the toll on people's lives would be severe. (The
process described here is already well underway in some colleges
and universities – hitting, as one would expect, the less presti-
gious ones first.)

The irony is that the institutions have not yet begun, in any
significant degree, to respond to the challenge facing them.
Instead, their administrators continue on with certificational
overextension, just through not knowing what else to do. As
a result, we are seeing some outright duplicity in the advertising
of these programs. Knowing privately that a given BA degree,
a specific, certificatory degree, is practically worthless in terms
of the market, some institutions imply to students in their
recruitment efforts that the jobs *will* be there. They know that
people who are shopping for a good buy in the academic
supermarket may be counted upon to be about as naive in
their consumer behavior as most of us are when shopping for
any "major purchase item" – an automobile, a refrigerator,
a house, and so on. They know, that is, that the facts stand a
good chance of not being checked out by the consumer. Most
people are unaware that institutions of higher education are
behaving in such predatory fashion; but times are tough, and
the institutions have vast human and monetary resources to
protect. (To their credit, some professional associations are
pressuring the colleges and universities to be honest about the

market relatedness of their curricula. The pressure is having a small but salutary effect.)

IV

In a time of inflation and dim job prospects, what are the people who used to go to college for economic reasons going to do when they graduate from high school? I believe that they ought to consider using such bad times to get themselves excellently educated. But they can be expected to do so only if the colleges begin to rededicate themselves to offering good liberal arts programs, and to advertising those programs well in their regions.

I think it is true that Americans have always been deeply in love with the idea of *the great education.* For most of them, sadly, it has been an unrequited love. We live in the best of times to say to them: "Take four years to educate yourself. Take even more. What else are you doing? What else are you going to do? All things considered, *you might as well learn."*

I have been saying those words to lots of students over the past six or seven years – to students who were thinking of leaving school because their hoped-for jobs were not going to be waiting for them. I have also said those words to retirees and others of middle age (and even old age) who were finding themselves, midway in the journey of their lives, wondering what in the world to do with those lives. In almost all cases, the words have seemed to wake the hearers up from a deep sleep. (In *all* cases, I have been told that no one else had said these words to them. Amazing.) The response is almost always the same (though it often takes a week or so of mulling over such a strange and revolutionary idea): "Yeah, *why not?"* They remembered the love they had forgotten.

V

But, even granting the existence of good curricula in the colleges and universities at the undergraduate level, a problem still remains: the course. The isolated course stands firmly in place, its position reinforced on all sides by the long-entrenched bureaucracies we call academic departments and divisions, themselves almost totally inappropriate to the needs of undergraduates who want and need to be well-educated. The course is best suited for the most basic kinds of skills-building work, as I have said, and for advanced work — graduate-level work — in a specialty area. Never mind that the skills-building work *ought* to take place in the high schools, and that the kinds of advanced work which call for specialized courses *ought* to take place at the doctoral level. I concede immediately that the high schools are not going to do that work as well as they should. The educationists have made the doing of that work impossible. (They now blame television.) And I concede that thousands of undergraduate professors will forever insist upon acting in their classrooms like publishing chair-holders in front-ranking graduate departments. I thus yield to the fact that the course cannot be gotten rid of in undergraduate education: it would be extremely naive to believe otherwise. But I do believe that its hold upon our curricular thinking can be lessened, and that its entrenchment in our institutions can now be made to give way to a better idea.

VI

Such a better idea has been around in the form of a strong model since the early 1920s. We first see it in a book by Alexander Meiklejohn called *The Liberal College.*

Meiklejohn's idea was that the liberal arts curriculum should be centered on the reading of some of the very best and most universal ancient and modern classics — the "best that has been thought and said." He put his theories into practice when he presided over the Experimental College at the University of Wisconsin from 1927 to 1932. The memory of this college in the minds of its graduates — most of whom are now around seventy, and many of whom are unusually distinguished in their fields — has served as a rallying point and a dream. The idea was not without curricular influence. It was part of the inspiration behind the St. John's College curriculum, which was described in persuasive detail in an important book which is now almost forgotten: Mark Van Doren's *Liberal Education.* In general form, it also found strong proponents in such educators as Robert M. Hutchins, Stringfellow Barr, Scott Buchanan, and Mortimer Adler, each of whom wrote widely about their versions of it.

Meiklejohn insisted from the beginning that his curriculum's rationale was the need for decision-making citizens in a democracy to be educated enough to take advantage of their freedoms — not just for their own individual sakes, but also for the sake of the society. If anything, this need is more urgent now than it was in the days of Meiklejohn and his college. Justice Burger, for example, argued in *The Christian Science Monitor* (24 August 1979) that most jurors today are simply unqualified to do their duty, as jurors' knowledge has not kept pace with the complexities of modern life, and hence of modern issues. The championing of such a curriculum is a particularly sensible response for the public sector — for the states.

But Meiklejohn also insisted on a second thing and it is this particular insistence which gives us a curricular invention which is far superior to the course for most undergraduate purposes. He demanded that the classroom "delivery" of the curriculum be interdisciplinary — that it deal with human issues, and not worry so much about specialized fields of expertise; the study of specialized fields would more usefully be reserved for those going on to graduate or professional schools. The *issues* are the important thing, Meiklejohn realized, and the isolated course is too narrow to deal with them well. Moreover, it hardly bears saying again that the world itself is not cut up into course-like strips. So it makes little sense to study it as if it were, especially when more important matters must go begging as a result.

Both demands added up to the need for carefully constructed, carefully sequenced programs of study, designed and taught by small teams of professors from various fields who would work closely with one another and with student seminars of reasonable size. Such programs of study, built around themes and issues, are especially viable now. There are two reasons why this is so.

The first is that we no longer live in the period — a period which came *after* Meiklejohn and which only recently died — when the course-structure in the liberal arts curriculum could find a rationale in the fact that many liberal arts students were preparing to be school teachers and college professors. Thus, there is no longer the need for sequenced course "coverage," as this coverage was meant to provide students with informational minutiae to be used in their own teaching. *They would need it in their own schooling, it was felt, because they, too, would be teaching future teachers!* We are now off the teacher-training treadmill, as it is not supported by markets at any instructional level, including the graduate school level. This may or may not be a good thing. It is, however, true. And it is going to remain true for a long time. (No argument should be seen here for less rigorous higher education. The argument is for more rigor, not less.)

The second reason is given by Richard Jones in this book, *Experiment at Evergreen:* as Meiklejohn also could not have foreseen, the structure of course/department/tenure came to produce, in the modern college and university, a vast syndrome of faculty boredom and "burnout." Interdisciplinary programs cause college teaching to remain exciting for those who come to teach for a long time. They do not eliminate "burnout"; but at least it occurs for better reasons, and institutions which stress interdisciplinary teaching can easily provide "alternative service" during some years for renewal and recreation – as well as for outright resuscitation. Jones makes the argument well.

VII

Meiklejohn, writing in the early twenties, also did not foresee that his curriculum would need, in our time, to make room for an excellent introduction to the natural sciences. Like many another humanist, he was blissfully unaware that by 1960 we would be living in the "two cultures" situation first identified as such by the late Lord Snow. That situation is still with us, though it shows signs of breaking down. I cannot sufficiently stress that its *creation* was due to the course/department state of affairs described above. That state of affairs was itself brought about by the poorest possible organizational response to the Renaissance by the faculties of European universities – a response copied by American universities. Meiklejohn's ideas, if now made to incorporate the sciences, provide a clear pathway to reintegration. It is ironic that it is really a "backward" pathway, one which would enable us to begin to establish in our institutions that which should have been established long, long ago. Better late than never.

VIII

The Experimental College at Madison was short-lived. Several attempts were made to revive it in other places, but none succeeded until the dream was adopted and nurtured by Joseph Tussman. In his *Experiment at Berkeley* (Oxford University Press, 1969), Tussman tells of his four-year chance to set up and run an experimental program almost exactly like Meiklejohn's. Tussman's experiment was also brief; and in part of his book he explains why. The problem was not the Meiklejohn curriculum. Rather, it was the individual, professional fear of leaving one's departmental niche, even briefly, to do the requisite collaborative teaching. Tussman simply could not find enough experienced professors on the Berkeley faculty who would risk participation in the experiment. (Such fear of risk-taking in higher education is rife, and I do not know to what extent the general public is aware of it. It is analogous to, if not the *same* as, bureaucratic behavior everywhere.)

Tussman's four-year try at resurrection was an important one. In the first place, it gave good educations to a fairly large number of students. In the second place, Tussman and his colleagues learned a great deal about how to do liberal arts teaching in an interdisciplinary, collaborative way. In the third place, the work produced the book *Experiment at Berkeley,* which, up until the present volume, was the only record of its kind in existence – not just for Tussman's particular experiment, but for any kind of interdisciplinary liberal arts experiment in American higher education. Fourth, *Experiment at Berkeley* came to play, almost by accident, a crucial role in the setting up of a much more solid experiment: The Evergreen State College.

IX

In 1967, the state of Washington set up a new four-year college. The state capital, Olympia, was chosen as the site. Administrators were hired and told to recruit a small and distinguished group of planning faculty. In was understood in the state that this new college was to be a different, nontraditional kind of institution, one which did not duplicate the other "regional" colleges. The planning faculty were given one year to decide what kind of college, specifically, it would be, and to have a curriculum ready when the first thousand students were to show up the following October. The deans and planning faculty were agreed that the new college should be one which would give the finest education possible to its students — and that it would give it to them at very lost costs. All other agreements remained to be reached.

One of the three deans chosen for the institution, by now named The Evergreen State College, was Mervyn Cadwallader. He was a disciple of Meiklejohn's and an ally of Tussman's. He had organized a program similar to Tussman's at San Jose State College. As the planning faculty were busily discussing the history of higher education and thinking hard about what to create (having been given virtual carte blanche), Cadwallader suggested that they read the Tussman book. They did so, and the rapid result was that the structural, stylistic, "delivery" features of the Meiklejohn-Tussman model were made the center of the Evergreen curriculum. Interdisciplinary programs would predominate.

The planning faculty did not, however, wholeheartedly commit to the "content" of the Meiklejohn-Tussman model. Too many ideologies were present in the room for that to happen; and all those competing ideologies, together with the utopian spirit which prevailed in the planning work, militated against any curricular conclusions which might be seen by planning members or factions as restrictive. Instead, curricular pluralism prevailed; but, even so, the Meiklejohn-Tussman *structure* was nailed firmly in place. That in itself was something — especially as the offering of the original Meiklejohn-Tussman curriculum was wholeheartedly encouraged.

The result was that Alexander Meiklejohn's structural model was not only living on, but was being committed to on a scale which would have exceeded even the wildest dreams of his followers the world over. The first thousand students *did* show up, and they were met with a curriculum unlike any offered before by a state institution on a large scale. Today,

LIBRARY-MEDIA CENTER
SOUTH PUGET SOUND COMM. COLLEGE
2011 MOTTMAN RD. S.W.
OLYMPIA, WA 98512-6292

041932

2500 students are here; and the past ten years have clearly demonstrated, I think, that what Richard Jones is calling "The Evergreen Experiment" is in most ways a successful one. It has shown that interdisciplinary education at the undergraduate level, when committed to by an entire institution, is an extremely realistic response to the modern world. (That it is an idealistic response goes without saying; but idealistic responses must be realistic in order to get anywhere in institutions.) It has also shown that Meiklejohn-Tussman programs in "great books" are tailor-made for a large number of today's students. We have offered a good many such programs since 1971, and all have been successful. We have yet to offer a complete four-year sequence in "great books" plus natural sciences, though individual students have been able, with ingenuity, to put one together for themselves. Yet, even though Evergreen has not bought into the Meiklejohn-Tussman curriculum to the exclusion of other kinds of interdisciplinary offerings, it has still invested in the idea more heavily than any other state-supported institution in America, and it remains the only place in the country where students can get Alexander Meiklejohn's kind of liberal arts education — for four years, if the student and his advisor will work to put it together — at state college prices.

X

Richard Jones was one of the members of the Evergreen planning faculty in 1970–71. He had left his position as Professor of Psychology at Harvard and Chief Psychologist of the Massachusetts Department of Mental Health in order to take part in the exciting work shaping up out in Olympia. After ten years, he is still at Evergreen, and he has a long string of distinguished Coordinated Studies programs behind him. Last year, he decided that it would be instructive to look at his college not just in terms of its own ten-year history as an American "experimental" college, but also in terms of its history as one of the three chapters in the overall experiment. He hopes for many future chapters.

Experiment at Evergreen is a slim book. Yet within its pages is an enormous amount of information about a *particular* alternative, a *particular* strategy for constructive change. Though

LIBRARY-MEDIA CENTER
SOUTH PUGET SOUND COMM. COLLEGE
2011 MOTTMAN RD. S.W.
OLYMPIA, WA 98512-6292

it is not a polemic, it is filled with drama. The drama has to do with the large stakes which are on the table in higher education. In this introduction, I have tried to do what Jones does not do – to gloss the drama for readers who are not academics. Jones aims his book primarily at an audience of tenured college and university professors – "insiders" of the first (and top) rank – in the hope of helping them see that they might yet have a way of reclaiming, in their actual classroom teaching, some of the ideals which animated them when they were just starting out. Speaking as one who has now done six years of the specific kind of collaborative liberal arts teaching Jones describes and recommends, I do hope with him that this target audience might be reached – and moved – by *Experiment at Evergreen*. Should this happen, nothing but good could come of it.

But my own hope is that this book be read by "outsiders"; for the sort of "insider" talk which goes on in these pages will be found by them to be accessible, and their attention to it ought to help them get a clearer picture of what is going on in higher education today. It can serve as a kind of wire-tap, if you will, through which a layperson can hear a succinct piece of history which is important to them. And one of the book's greatest uses, in my view, is that it can give nonacademics a look and a listen into domains which still today remain cloistered. The internal workings of colleges and universities have been largely unknown to the general public since the very beginnings of such institutions in the West, *circa* 1100. Yet, even though the beginnings of large-scale public funding of higher education are now over a century behind us, the monastic walls still remain. I am personally not sure that those walls should be torn down. But I am more and more certain that they *will* be. Taxpayers are suddenly aware of how much the institutions cost, and they are suddenly interested in where all the money is going. They are thus suddenly demanding "accountability," which in turn is proving difficult for legislators to provide. Legislators have been passing elephantine academic budgets for at least fifty years; but they know almost nothing about the curricular debates of colleges and universities, save perhaps for those few who make themselves expert through serving on higher education committees; and those few know how daunting the acquisition of such expertise can be. The point is that curricular debates produce all other debates. Hence, they produce all questions of funding.

Cloister or no cloister, it is important that citizens know of the option provided by the Meiklejohn-Tussman experiment and of its spirited survival at The Evergreen State College. I believe, as does Jones, that it is an experiment which should be enlarged. If so, it will have to be judged good enough to supplant existing curricula elsewhere. That means that it will have to be judged good enough to win funding. As funding is done by nonacademics, we immediately have a compelling reason for widening our curricular debate to include them. (Another excellent reason is that the debate is itself intrinsically educational — and always has been.) We can only expect that inquiries similar to those which led to the nationwide "back-to-basics" movement a year or two ago will soon be probing higher education. I think that we "insiders" should welcome such outside scrutiny — *if* we are ready with good rebuttals to the "college-is-mainly-for-a-job" prejudice. Richard Jones' book provides a close-up picture which was unavailable to citizens before — not about one college *per se,* but about a workable but little-known strategy for giving undergraduates an excellent education. I hope that it will interest laypersons in our heretofore restricted debate. I hope, too, that it will provide them with some new ideas which, along with ideas gleaned from other good sources, might enable them to make wise decisions about the tough problems in higher education likely to face them soon. When they come to the fore, those problems are going to be more public than ever before. I also hope, as will surprise no one who has read this far, that *Experiment at Evergreen* will be a planted seed which eventually will make "great books" partisans of them. But, even if not, the important thing is that nonacademics begin to study the issues at a deep enough level to permit understanding and to promote educated decision making.

This is what Alexander Meiklejohn wanted books to do — and citizens to do with them.

Leo Daugherty
Faculty of Literature and Linguistics
The Evergreen State College

1

THE MEIKLEJOHN-TUSSMAN CONNECTION

In the autumn of 1970 a small book, *Experiment at Berkeley* (Oxford University Press, 1969) by Joseph Tussman, was read and discussed by eighteen men who had been brought to Olympia, Washington, to design an alternative college, The Evergreen State College. This experience was to have a decisive influence on the development of one of the most revealing experiments in the history of American higher education. Tussman's experimental program was modeled on Alexander Meiklejohn's Experimental College at the University of Wisconsin. Both experiments were short-lived. Meiklejohn's lasting from 1927 to 1932; Tussman's from 1965 to 1969. Compared to that of its progenitors, the Evergreen experiment with what we have called programs of coordinated study has had a long and varied life.

Both irony and serendipity suffuse this Meiklejohn-Tussman-Evergreen lineage. Tussman was primarily attracted to Meiklejohn's model on *curricular* grounds: its concern with "initiation in the great political vocation," and he sought to achieve this objective by way of studying some of the seminal works of classical Greece, seventeenth-century England, and the United States Supreme Court. It was not, however, the *curricular*

21

innovation of these two men which claimed the imaginations of the Evergreen planning faculty in 1970. What influenced us most was the *pedagogical* innovation which both men introduced in order to achieve their curricular objectives: substituting for the traditional format of separate teachers, teaching separate courses, in separated blocks of time, to separate groups of students (who are separately combining different assortments of courses), a format in which *a team of teachers teach the same group of students, who are all studying the same things at the same time, over a prolonged period.*

With neither Tussman's purposes, nor the Evergreen planning faculty's intentions having much to do with the matter (enter the serendipity), the following observation of Tussman's was, in retrospect, the main hypothesis which the Evergreen experiment was designed to test:

> While the Program has been conceived from the beginning as an integral whole, it is possible to distinguish two aspects: its curriculum or "subject," and its pedagogic structure. Each is an important part of the experiment, but it has always been considered possible that the general structure might commend itself to some who would not approve of the particular curriculum and who might wish to experiment with something like the same form and a quite different curriculum. (*Experiment at Berkeley*, p. 109.)

The irony is compounded by the fact that few of the present Evergreen faculty, which now numbers 126, know of the Meiklejohn and Tussman experiments, much less that the unusual conditions in which they find themselves working were prefigured by them. Indeed, Tussman's book is now dim in the memories of the Evergreen planning faculty; some even deny that it had a significant influence on their thoughts during the planning process. The undeniable facts are, though, that all but one of the eighteen planning faculty, and all but one of the thirty-seven faculty recruited for the college's first operational year, either chose or were assigned to teach in a program of coordinated study. None of these programs followed the Meiklejohn-Tussman *curricular* model; all of them followed the Meiklejohn-Tussman *pedagogic* model. Although there was no agreed-upon intention to test Tussman's hypothesis, that is precisely what we did, and have largely been doing, with constantly changing curricular variations, for ten years — with results that have revealed entirely new conceptions of what it can mean to go to college and what it can mean to teach in college.

Actually, so prominent in his book is Tussman's emphasis on the curricular aspects of the Berkeley experiment, and so low-key is his description of its pedagogical aspects, that it was easy for the Evergreen planners to forget the impact that the book obviously had, especially since none chose to replicate Tussman's curricular design. Not that we disapproved of the design; simply, none of us particularly wished, at that time, to study the seminal works of classical Greece, seventeenth-century England, and the United States Supreme Court.

Another factor probably entered into the forming of this step-lineage: In other discussions and meetings, the Evergreen planners managed to paint the prospective college out of so many traditional corners that little room was left for the imagination of anything but something like the Meiklejohn-Tussman pedagogic model. It would be hard for an historian to accurately trace Evergreen's departures from traditional forms to their origins. The enabling legislation merely charged that the new college not be a duplicate of its three established sisters, and that it serve the educational needs of the southwest quadrant of the state. The college's first president, Charles McCann, while strongly committed to the college being an innovative one, imposed no particular innovations of his own. Three academic deans were recruited from the three traditional academic divisions. Each of these had directed experimental programs at other institutions. One dean, Mervyn Cadwallader, emerged as Evergreen's first acknowledged visionary, on the strength of his very strongly held and very articulate ideas of what our *positive* academic objectives should be. Cadwallader was a follower of Meiklejohn, and had directed a program at San Jose State College which closely resembled Tussman's.*

The eighteen members of the planning faculty, which were

---

*There is no published account of this program.

given the academic year of 1970–71 to design the college's specific policies and programs, were recruited on the basis of their interest and experience in experimental education of a variety of types: Great Books, Humanistic, Self-Paced, Affective, Outward Bound, Cooperative, and Cadwallader's program at San Jose State. From such a range of backgrounds and interests, little lasting agreement was likely to emerge in positive matters of philosophy; and, in fact, no such lasting agreement did emerge. What did was a rather hastily achieved negative consensus: the college would have no requirements, no grades, no majors and no departments. What would take the place of these? Something in which students would be given a larger than usual share of responsibility for designing and evaluating their education; something in which the various academic disciplines would be related as well as covered; something in which greater emphasis would be placed on how to learn than on what to learn.

It was to this highly charged and almost recklessly ambiguous set of untested intentions that Cadwallader introduced Evergreen's planning faculty to Tussman's *Experiment at Berkeley*. His own intention was modest. He hoped that a few of the planning faculty would find the Tussman program sufficiently appealing to design it into the college's curriculum. Like Tussman, Cadwallader was infatuated with the curricular aspects of the program. "The Moral Curriculum," he called it. He was, at the time, writing a book about it. The program's pedagogic design features were to him, as to Tussman, merely the optimal means to the achievement of the moral curriculum's end: "initiation into the great political vocation." To Cadwallader's chagrin, none of the planning faculty went on to include the moral curriculum in the first year's offerings. To his probable astonishment, all but one of the planning faculty went on to design a program based on the structural features of the Tussman program.

What astonishes me, now, is the recognition of how dimly conscious we were at the time that we were actually following a written prescription. It is impossible to describe the turbulence that went into the development of a college which sought to put alternatives in the place of requirements, grades, majors, departments and (having opted to follow Tussman's prescription) courses. Only a small part of the planning year could go into the shaping of specific academic programs. There were 37 new faculty to be selected from over 7,000 applicants. Admissions, evaluation and registration policies and procedures had to be devised. A faculty handbook had to be written, and dozens of decisions made as to how the faculty should conduct and govern itself, before the handbook could be written. (As it went, we also opted against faculty rank and tenure.) Buildings had to be designed. Policies and procedures for public relations, student housing, advising, counseling, financial aid, and administration had to be formed.

In the rush of readying the college for its first 1,000 students in the fall of 1971, it is understandable (though still remarkable) that we almost overlooked what an historian would have seen to be our primary mission: to further develop an educational strategy which was first tried at the University of Wisconsin in the 1920s, and then at San Jose State, and at Berkeley just a few years before we came to Olympia. Had it not been for a long letter that I wrote to a friend and former colleague midway through the planning year, I would myself have forgotten the Meiklejohn-Tussman connection. The following excerpts from the letter will convey something of the mood of Evergreen's planning year:

February 17, 1971

Dr. Jack Michaelsen
Professor of Economics
University of California
Santa Cruz, California 95060

Dear Jack:

I have been looking for an occasion to commit to paper my impressions of The Evergreen State College at this embryonic stage in its development. As you know, it becomes increasingly difficult, with time, to maintain the clear long view on such ventures, and I've been wanting to memorialize current impressions for future reference, but have not been able to get myself to write to a file cabinet. So thanks for sending *Assessing the*

Benefits of Collegiate Structure: The Case at Santa Cruz. Not only does it provide your personal commitments to educational reform as points for me to talk to, but it raises many important spectra along which Evergreen may be usefully compared.

First, an overall impression: where Santa Cruz has sought to adopt positions of compromise between novel and traditional ways (positions of "dynamic tension" I believe McHenry has called them) with respect to administrative structures and functions, educational policy, teaching and research emphases, student and faculty recruitment, and student and faculty evaluation; Evergreen appears to be going for broke on the side of innovative policies and practices. Everything we are planning has been tried before in one way or another, but usually as isolated experiments in otherwise traditional settings. I know of nothing like the particular combination we are planning, nor of so total an institutional commitment to a new direction. This, I think will prove to be at once our greatest vulnerability as an institution and our greatest value as an experiment. . . .

My major reservation at the top is the probably unreasonable one that McCann is not a Meiklejohn. He has shaped a quite modest legislative mandate of purely local reference (to build a new State College which is not a carbon copy of others existing in the State of Washington) into a sweepingly innovative effort of national significance. But in this McCann is more negatively than positively inspired. In this connection we are fortunate in having as one of our deans a close follower of Meiklejohn and Tussman. This man has supplied much of the imagination and initiative for much of what we are planning to do positively in the first years. . . .

Santa Cruz and Evergreen share the same negative objective in that they both seek to avoid organization by departments. Where the two institutions differ is in the length to which each is prepared to go, and the risks each is prepared to take, in order to secure this avoidance.

About the only thing we have not done to preclude the emergence of departmentalization at Evergreen is to take oaths in blood. No Boards of Studies, no Institutes, no institutionalized affiliation by professional discipline of any kind. Furthermore, although there are more positive reasons for these, no graduate programs in the first two years, no simultaneous faculty involvement in graduate and undergraduate programs at any time, no majors, no courses, no concentration requirements, no breadth requirements.

In place of these familiar forms we plan to offer two kinds of programs: Coordinated Studies and Contracted Studies. Coordinated studies programs are multi-disciplinary, and are organized in such ways as to make it unlikely that a faculty member will be teaching in the content area of his expertise more than a small portion of the time. These programs require students and teachers to develop the skills necessary to work effectively toward common objectives as members of groups, and will encourage the generalizing aspects of the learning process. Contracted study may be undertaken individually or in small groups. These programs are designed to meet the more specialized needs of students and faculty. . . .

The attendant risks of our curricular organization are several. The main one is at the level of administration. Obviously, two authority vacuums are being created here: 1) the authority of expertise traditionally exerted by departments and department heads, which has traditionally ordered faculty responsibilities; and 2) the authority of rule as carried by curricular requirements, which has traditionally ordered student responsibilities. How these vacuums are eventually filled will tell the Evergreen story more than anything else. . . .

Now to your references to Tussman:

The basic structure of our coordinated studies programs follows Tussman's model almost to the letter: multidisciplinary, theme-oriented, total engagement of five faculty and 100 students, small intensive seminars, common reading list and schedule. However, in using this structure over a much wider range of thematic areas, we expect it to achieve a wider set of goals. Also, by committing a major part of our resources to this model, we hope to avoid some of the problems that Tussman has at Berkeley. The Experimental Program at Berkeley is really one coordinated studies program, functioning as a tiny enclave in a large traditional setting, as was Meiklejohn's Experimental

College at Wisconsin. We will offer ten coordinated studies program options to our 1,000 students when we open next September, and as our population increases, so will the number of coordinated studies. Tussman seems almost to prize the substance of his program more than its structure. While we like the substance of his program, and plan to offer one much like it someday, it is the pedagogical power of the structure that we prize most, and are therefore applying it over a wide range of substantive areas. . . .

As for the problem of finding effective incentives to induce a professionalized faculty to make serious commitments to a liberal arts program, which plagues Tussman at Berkeley and the College programs at Santa Cruz, maybe we are being incredibly naive but we aren't expecting any such problem at Evergreen. We simply propose not to offer any enduring alternatives. Therefore, faculty members who need special inducements to make this commitment will either not come to Evergreen or not stay. . . .

As mentioned in the letter, programs of coordinated study were not the only instructional format designed by the planning faculty. Group contracts were to be offered, in which fifteen to twenty students would work full-time with one faculty member in order to pursue intensive studies of specialized kinds. Advanced students, prepared to study independently with minimal faculty supervision, would be invited to propose programs of independent study under the rubric of individual learning contracts. However, the opening year of the college saw fifty of its fifty-two faculty working in teams of from three to seven in the following programs of coordinated study:*

    Causality, Freedom and Chance
    Contemporary American Minorities
    Human Development

---

*Each of these was a liberal arts curriculum, defined by Meiklejohn as one in which "instruction is dominated by no special interest, is limited by no single human task, but is intended to take human activity as a whole, to understand human endeavors not in their isolation but in their relations to one another and to the total experience which we call the life of our people." (*The Liberal College*, 1920.)

The Individual in America
The Individual, the Citizen and th
Political Ecology
Human Behavior
Space, Time and Form: Common Problem
  Science
Environmental Design
Man and Art: The Renaissance and Now

The first year in the development of an institution,
first year in the development of a person, prefigures its futu
some fundamental ways. Evergreen's first year of experien
was that of almost its entire faculty seeking to adapt their
individual styles, habits, biases and preconceptions to conditions of collaboration which none but the small San Jose
contingent had ever experienced, and which had never before
been attempted on such a scale. For some, the experience was
debilitating; for others it was exhilarating; for almost all, it
was tantalizing. Teaching, we had all been taught, was, by defi-
nition, a strictly private enterprise and here we were all trying
to do it together under each others' noses. The year ended on
the unanimous agreement that, if we were to go on this way, we
all had a lot to learn. The differences that had tended to divide
us in the planning year – the mutual antipathy of the humanistic education and great books champions, the chauvinism with
which community internships were regarded by some, the suspi-
cions held by others as to the place of wilderness experiences in
an academic community, the derision with which affective
education was regarded by still others – became trivialities before the commonly felt excitement of having tried for a year to
find out how groups of professors could teach effectively, for
whatever purposes, *together.* It was an unforgettable experience
in the life of the college, and it continues to influence the
institution's reactions to unforeseen circumstances. For example, as we find ourselves, today, scrambling to solve an
underenrollment crisis by way of reinventing traditional forms
under futuristic names ("specialty areas" and "specialty area
convenors" for departments and department heads; "career
tracks" for majors; "modules" for courses; "embedded modules" for part-time courses) we find the college's second

State

s in Art and

ike the
re in
ce

)an Evans, writing to

so far, and many of
en more understand-
inity. I believe most
tain the core of Ever-
ind interdisciplinary
an competitive edu-

hn or Tussman, and
;ram of coordinated
:ician, an intelligent
... ... a uioughtful citizen; and I interpret this reminder to the Evergreen faculty as his response to a generative educational concept which, although it has taken sixty years for it to barely survive in this country, is of significant societal value. That value, as I have come to perceive it, lies in its recognition that the liberal mind needs exercise in collective as well as private enterprise. Commitment to this value requires that we radically depart from established societal assumptions and educational practices, as was stated by Tussman as follows:

> A sustained attempt to improve the quality of education reveals, as perhaps nothing else does, how deeply we, as a society, are imbued with the ideas and attitudes of competitive individualism. We do not really think of man as a political animal or even understand what that means. We think of him as essentially a private person created, by God or by himself, complete with mind, self, goals, rights — autonomous and naturally sovereign over himself. All relations are foreign relations, entered into for private reasons, justified in private terms. . . . So we remain individualists. Children of the polis, we deny our generative source and then enjoy our crisis of identity. We search for ourselves in all the wrong places. (*Experiment at Berkeley*, pp. 65–66.)
>
> The course forces teaching into small, relatively self-contained units. Horizontally, courses are generally unrelated and competitive. That is, the student is taking three or four or even five courses simultaneously. They are normally in different subjects, given by different

professors, and, with rare exceptions, there is no attempt at horizontal integration. Thus, each professor knows that he has a valid claim to only a small fraction of a student's time and attention. The effect is that no teacher is in a position to be responsible for, or effectively concerned with, the student's total educational situation. The student presents himself to the teacher in fragments, and not even the advising system can put him together again.

What is worse is that the professor knows that even his fragment of the student's time must be competitively protected. If he does not make tangible, time-consuming demands the student diverts time to courses which do make such demands. It becomes almost impossible to set a reflective, contemplative, deliberate pace in a single course. The tendency is to over-assign work, with the expectation that it will probably not all be done. The cumulative effect on the student is brutal. To survive he must learn how to not do his work; he is forced into the adoption of the strategies of studentship; he learns to read too fast, to write and speak with mere plausibility. His educational life, through no fault of his own, becomes a series of artificial crises. (*Experiment at Berkeley,* p. 5.)

The two quotations reveal the basic links between the Berkeley and the Evergreen experiments; both questioned the societal values of competitive individualism and both, therefore, challenged the tacit presumptions that going to college means taking courses and that teaching in college means giving courses.

Programs of coordinated study now comprise only about half of Evergreen's total curriculum, and those that continue are under mounting pressure to do so on less than a full-time basis. The causes of this development are too complex to try to identify now, and would require another book, and are, anyway, irrelevant to the purpose of this report: to record what became of the Meiklejohn-Tussman-Cadwallader concept during its life here in Olympia from 1970 to 1980.

2

DIFFERENCES AND COMMONALITIES

The experiment at Berkeley was a tiny one, conducted tentatively, with the ambivalent sponsorship of a large established university. Evergreen is a small state college, committed to collaborative teaching as its primary mission. This difference has had an interesting bearing on the problem of program staffing. For Tussman, this loomed as the most recalcitrant problem. How to persuade faculty members to leave their departmental niches to engage in an experimental form of teaching which can be nothing but its own reward? Berkeley faculty are recruited on the basis of singular interests and records of achievement in a given discipline. And they have usually been attracted to Berkeley by the prospect of doing research in concert with colleagues of similar disciplinary zeal. To expect young untenured faculty to join his "nondisciplinary" program would have been, as Tussman points out, both unreasonable and counterproductive. He hoped, rather, that enough senior faculty would find the prospect of pursuing wisdom instead of knowledge, for a finite period, sufficiently appealing to keep the program going. The hope proved to be unrealistic.

The staffing problem at Evergreen has been the opposite. All of our faculty have been recruited on the basis of *interest* in collaborative teaching. However, because of the obvious impossibility of selecting for *experience* in collaborative teaching, all of our faculty appointments have been risks. One risk is that of the faculty candidate who succeeds in persuading us that he is dying to engage in collaborative teaching but who is secretly plotting to be near the Pacific Northwest's ski slopes. Another risk is the person who is similarly persuasive, who at heart merely wants a job — *any* job. The more frequent mismatch has been the person who is genuinely attracted to the rhetoric of collaborative teaching, and who genuinely believes he will enjoy learning how to do it, but who, when faced with the realities of its unusual demands, finds that he hates it. Finally, there is the person who is given an unfortunate first assignment in a program that fails. (Tussman's program was a success in that it stayed intact through its planned period of existence, and retained a large percentage of its students. Most of Evergreen's programs have also been successful by these minimal criteria, but some have not been; and one addition we are able to make to the Berkeley findings is that failure in a program of coordinated study is an enervating professional trauma. A few of our failures have been outright, with the faculty members openly admitting they could not continue working together and having, consequently, to renege on their commitments to the students — leaving everyone to scramble in search of alternative commitments in a limited field of options at an awkward time. A small number of teams have failed by not admitting their incompatibilities and limping through the motions of collaborative teaching, with the faculty being ashamed and the students (those who stay) being confused. The cause of the failures has consistently been the same: unresolvable faculty team incompatibility. The scope of Evergreen's commitment to coordinated study has thus had the drawback that it forced underestimation of the importance of careful program staffing. Tussman unabashedly says that the faculty team should include some personal friends. So far from this ideal have we had to move at Evergreen that we have risked some programs which were staffed by people who had not met before being assigned to work together. Our best successes bear Tussman out. They were programs that were designed and taught by teams which included personal friends. Some potential failures have been avoided by the guidance of team members with previous successful experience in other programs. We have found that launching a program with a faculty team consisting of inexperienced strangers is a very foolish gamble.

Having to function within the University of California's system of requirements and departmental majors, Tussman and his team had to settle for three-fourths of the students' time. At Evergreen we have been able to assume that the students in a program of coordinated study have no other claims on their energies but those placed on them by their program.*

Another difference has to do with the focus of faculty frustration. Tussman's team had to be concerned with how its activities were perceived by the Berkeley faculty at large, whose patronage was necessary if the experiment was to continue. Thus, Tussman had to make regular reports on the program's progress to appropriate faculty committees. At Evergreen, where the majority of the faculty are working in teams, lack of communication between the teams has been a source of frustration. Each program develops an idiomatic life of its own, sometimes evolving its own vocabulary for discussing its particular problems. Aside from there being little time for shop talk between faculty teams, there is often not the background of intimate knowledge necessary for the shop talk to be informative. Horror stories and misleading rumors can be hard to squelch. Pride in one's work can only be shared in a very small circle.

Student ambience was also different. Although Tussman's program had its own exclusive space (a converted fraternity house on the edge of the Berkeley campus), it never became a center of intellectual and social activity for most of its students. How much of this was due to the students being concurrently

---

*This was a safe assumption during the early years; it has become less so as the college has sought to respond to its other mandate: to serve the citizens of Southwest Washington. Many students are attracted to the college not because of its innovative mission but because of its location, and, in a time of declining enrollment, we have had to yield to some pressures which preclude full-time commitment. However, a number of our programs continue to be offered on a full-time basis.

enrolled in a separate course cannot be known. I suspect that the larger cause was the students' identifying themselves as University students and Berkeley residents first, and as members of the Experimental Program second. Most of their friends were taking courses, and were they to become dissatisfied with the program, the option to go back to taking courses was readily available. (That so many stayed in the program for its full two years under these circumstances must have been a source of pride for Tussman and his colleagues.) Evergreen students live on or near a small campus on the outskirts of a small city. Their friends are not taking courses; they are either in the same program or they are in another program. Under these circumstances, an Evergreen program tends to become the primary ambient within which its students center their intellectual, social and personal lives. A certain amount of switching from program to program can and does go on (this, too, is increasing) but this is not something that one does casually. There is the obstacle of having to catch up with the work of the other program. There is also the reluctance to leave your friends in midstream, even when you feel that your educational interests are not being well served.

There were also differences in clientele. Tussman's program was a strictly lower division program. All of its students began as first-year students, and when they completed the program, they reentered the university as juniors pursuing majors in various departments. Evergreen's programs have been offered at all levels: basic, intermediate and advanced. Moreover, because the college has no system of requirements, first-year students have applied and been admitted into intermediate and advanced programs; and second, third and fourth year students have applied and been admitted into basic and intermediate programs. Thus, while most of the students in a basic program have been in their first or second year, they have usually been joined by a sprinkling of third and fourth year students; and while most of the students in an advanced program have been in their third or fourth year, they have usually been joined by a sprinkling of first and second year students. This has made for a certain amount of administrative messiness, but from an educational point of view, it has been beneficial. Students, it seems, like to help each other when they have to.

Tussman's was a two-year program. Most of Evergreen's have been one-year programs. The student-faculty ratio at Berkeley was 30 to 1 (150 students and 5 faculty) which attrition reduced to 20 to 1 in the second year. Evergreen's programs are targeted to function at a 20 to 1 ratio, which attrition usually reduces to about 15 to 1 by the program's third quarter. Evergreen programs have been designed for a variety of combinations within the 20 to 1 parameter; from 40 students and 2 faculty to 140 students and 7 faculty.

The Berkeley experiment proscribed student participation in program planning. Tussman is at his polemical best on this point:

> . . . The view of the college as a political democracy is nonsense. It may be, at this time, unconquerable nonsense, but it is nonsense none the less. Of course, a college is really not "undemocratic" either. The concept is simply inapplicable. . . . "Democracy" applied to a college makes about as much sense as "democracy" applied to a rainbow or to a baseball game.

At Evergreen we have had to live with a lot of this nonsense at the level of talk, but we have largely succeeded in avoiding it at the level of action. The college's gestation period (1967–71) coincided with the height of the "participatory democracy" push by college students across the land. A new and innovative college could hardly have opened then without being perceived by many as being committed to student participation in all aspects of its development. Especially when one of the leading innovations consisted of giving students a larger share of responsibility for designing and evaluating their education. This was, and continues to be, interpreted by a vocal minority of Evergreen students to mean that they should also be responsible for designing the education of *other* students. Every year there has been some kind of political move by some students to become involved in curriculum planning, and some members of the faculty and administration have sought to respond to it. In actuality, the involvement of students in program design has been negligible. When invited to help design a program, most of the students find that they have neither the knowledge nor the time for it, and lose interest. The students in a successful program quickly realize, with gratitude, that its design would never have occurred to them. Thus, the Evergreen experience confirms Tussman's observation that designing a program of study, which will support collaborative teaching and learning, is an exacting art, the practice of which requires a good deal of experience in both learning and teaching.

From an historical point of view, and in the interest of husbanding the Evergreen experience for future reference, the commonalities of the Berkeley and Evergreen experiments are more instructive than their differences. In both, teams of faculty drawn from different disciplines committed their teaching efforts exclusively to the same group of students, whose commitments, in turn, were either exclusively or primarily to a common program of study. In both, books and subjects were read and studied not as ends in themselves, but as means toward exploring an interesting theme or problem which no single discipline could articulate. (Some Evergreen programs have substituted for the integrative theme or problem — or added to it — an integrative project, such as writing a book, doing a survey, giving a performance or mounting an exhibition.)

Both required that everyone keep to the same schedule of readings, writings, seminars and lectures. In both, the schedule sought to encourage the skills of unhurried, reflective learning. That is, for both, the learning was only part of the plan; enjoying the learning was the other part.

Both experiments discovered that this kind of communal learning puts a natural and comfortable premium on the development of communication skills. Learning to read with care, to write with style, to speak one's thoughts, and to listen skillfully, are not extraneous chores to be sweated in order to pass tests when the prevailing test is whether or not you have made yourself understood to your friends and whether or not you have succeeded in understanding them. When you remove the element of competition from the learning of communication skills, in other words, desist from perceiving them as "tools," and instead, create a communal setting in which mutual understanding is the first priority, developing skills in reading, writing and verbal discourse become the compelling sources of pride that they presumably were, for awhile, in childhood.

Faculty, too, benefit from the communal arrangements of coordinated study. You write a more artful evaluation of a student's work when you know that the student will share it with his friends in your seminar than you do when you are writing it to a student in the isolation of a course. And you give a more thoughtful lecture when you know that your teaching colleagues will be in the audience along with the students.

Effective collaborative teaching, of the kind involved in both the Berkeley and Evergreen experiments, required the same reorientation to one's discipline: you must resist the temptation to *teach* your subject – in favor of trying to *represent* it – in order that optimal interdisciplinary leverage may be applied to the program's theme, problem or project.

Finally, both experiments came to the same conclusion as to a program's most important design feature: the faculty seminar. Tussman described the faculty seminar as follows:

> Once each week, through the entire academic year, the faculty met for dinner and discussion. Mostly we discussed the program reading, argued about the ideas involved, and considered their educational significance. In spite of the heat which was sometimes generated, these meetings – which normally lasted about four hours – were delightful and exciting. The seminar shaped and supported the lecture program, brought out the issues, and made individual experience and insight the common property of the program. It is not too much to say that, in fact, the seminar *made* the program.

I shall have more to say about faculty seminars in a later chapter. Suffice to note that the Berkeley program was less successful before instituting regular faculty seminars than it was after doing so. And that, in Evergreen's history, those programs which failed either did not hold faculty seminars or discontinued holding them. Those programs which managed to struggle through the year more or less successfully were ones in which faculty seminars were dutifully held, because the founding fathers said that they should be. The most noteworthy of Evergreen's successes have been those programs whose faculty teams regarded the faculty seminar as the most important of its design features, who held it religiously and learned to enjoy it as the highlight of each work week.

Here are the descriptions of a very small sample of Evergreen's successful programs, as they appeared in the students' transcripts:

HUMAN DEVELOPMENT
Fall, Winter and Spring Quarters, 1977-78

The primary objectives of the program were to learn how to read with discrimination, to write with style and to think with clarity — individually and collectively. We chose to pursue these objectives while learning as much as we could of those aspects of the social sciences and the humanities which speak to the subject of human development. The two basic dimensions of human development which concerned us were the individual and the socio-historical dimensions. Thus, our theme: the dialectic of overlapping generations.

Psychohistory is an emerging new discipline in the social sciences. It seeks to combine the separate disciplines of psychology and history (among other social sciences) so as to be able to better understand the ways in which a person's social and historical milieu influences his or her individual development, and (sometimes) vice versa.

The work of the autumn quarter was directed toward preparing students for the central project of winter quarter: the writing of a psychohistorical study of one of one's parents. There were four components of this preparation.

First, we worked at mastering one particular framework for viewing human development: that of Erik Erikson. To appreciate both the strengths and weaknesses of the psychoanalytic tradition in which Erikson writes we read Freud's *Clark Lectures, Delusion and Dream,* and *The History of the Psychoanalytic Movement,* as well as Juliet Mitchell's *Psycho-analysis and Feminism.* We spent the major part of the quarter reading the bulk of Erikson's work: *Childhood and Society, Insight and Responsibility, Young Man Luther,* and *Gandhi's Truth.*

Second, we used the reading of literature as a vehicle for discussing our program theme. To this purpose we read: Conrad's *Heart of Darkness,* Miller's *A View from the Bridge,* Sophocles' *Oedipus Rex, Oedipus at Colonus,* and *Antigone,* Euripides'

Electra, The Phoenician Women, and *The Bacchae,* Shakespeare's *Hamlet* and *King Lear* and Hawthorne's *The Scarlet Letter.*

The psychology and literature were discussed and assimilated through films, lectures, seminars and workshops throughout the quarter. Students regularly wrote papers. In addition, two exams were given: a lengthy take-home exam at mid-quarter, and a comprehensive final exam.

Third, we used weekly "dream reflection seminars" as a vehicle for the improvement of expressive writing, and to give experience applying the specific ideas of psychological theory to concrete personal data. In preparation for this work, we read Richard Jones' *The Dream Poet.* The seminar is actually a 6–7 hour workshop, consisting of 2 meetings and an intervening period of intensive writing. The goal of the writing is to interrelate themes or imagery from the dream under discussion with the piece of literature being studied that week.

Fourth, the last month of the quarter was devoted in part to producing a series of specific guidelines for the collecting of the data for the psychohistory project (over winter break).

The primary thrust of winter quarter was the student's production of a finished first draft of the psychohistory of their parent, the main project for the year. About half of the work of the quarter was devoted to getting this work started. A series of four all-day workshops helped the students with basic expository writing skills in conjunction with assisting them in finding a theme or focus for their paper, interpreting their data (gathered through interview over winter break), beginning the paper, and organizing the parts of it. The students spent the rest of their time during these two weeks writing.

The study of literature in psychohistorical perspective continued through the more intensive study of two authors. We read Kafka's *The Metamorphosis, The Judgment,* and his autobiographical *Letter to his Father,* and Joseph Heller's *Something Happened.*

We completed our study of individual psychology early in the quarter through the study of Andras Angyal's conceptions of health and neurosis as contained in his *Neurosis and Treatment.* We then began a new component, an inquiry into the American character structure through a study of history and sociology. This component was intended to provide a historical dimension to our heretofore psychological view of "psychohistory." In this connection we read de Tocqueville's *Democracy in America; The Pursuit of Loneliness,* by Philip Slater; *White Racism: A Psychohistory* by Joel Kovel; Leuchtenburg's *F.D.R. and the New Deal;* and Studs Terkel's *Working.* As previously, the ideas in all the books were assimilated through a combination of seminars, lectures, workshops, and writing assignments. Creative writing continued through dream reflection seminars for some students and creative writing workshops for others.

Midway through the quarter, we had an evaluation week, in which all students and faculty wrote self-evaluations, and each student and his faculty adviser wrote evaluations of each other. These documents were discussed in individual conferences.

The main objectives of spring quarter were the students' completion of the final draft of their year-long project, the psychohistory of their parent, and the gradual integration and synthesis of the year's course of study in relation to the program theme, "the dialectic of overlapping generations." Psychohistory workshops continued for half the quarter, and were replaced by dream reflection seminars for some students and regular writing workshops for others. As before, other modes of study were book seminars, lectures, films, workshops and writing assignments.

The study of human development in psychohistorical perspective continued by reading an anthropologist's view of changing intergenerational relationships in Margaret Mead's *Culture and Commitment* and a social historian's view of the effect of advertising on the generations in America after 1920 in Stewart Ewen's *Captains of Consciousness.* We also looked at the implications of psychoanalytic theory for the "progress" of civilization in Freud's classic, *Civilization and its Discontents* and Norman O. Brown's inquiry, *Life Against Death.*

We took a slightly new approach to our theme this quarter by studying two contrasting autobiographies: Mark Vonnegut's *The Eden Express* and Simone de Beauvoir's *Memoirs of a Dutiful Daughter,* the first the story of an American male youth in the late 1960's, the second the story of a French female's young life in the early part of the 20th century.

Finally, we continued the study of literature, reading Whitman's long poem, *Song of Myself;* Faulkner's novel, *The Sound and the Fury; A Good Man is Hard to Find,* a collection of short stories by Flannery O'Connor; and Melville's *Moby Dick.*

We ended the year by rereading. We looked again at some of Erikson's ideas about human development, reading selections from his *Identity: Youth and   Crisis,* and we reread Shakespeare's *King Lear,* considering how our own intellectual development over the year had affected our understanding of the play.

DEMOCRACY AND TYRANNY:
THE PARADOX OF FREEDOM
One year (1973-74)

The program was dedicated to careful reading, good writing, and thoughtful conversation. It was to be a search for our roots in the past, an attempt to understand the present, and an analysis of our hopes and fears, for the future. We asked tough questions about our proper relationship to the state, to our community, and to ourselves. Even as we studied our heritage, we asked whether it was worth studying and whether our traditions are worth saving. We compared democratic Athens and America, imperialistic Athens and America, and creative Athens and America. The problems we studied were the problems of freedom and slavery, men and women, peace and war, courage and cowardice, good and evil, the beautiful and the ugly. Ancient Athens was the place where many of our values and most of our art started. Is all of that worth knowing and using today? Our conclusion was that it is.

REQUIRED ACTIVITIES FOR ALL STUDENTS
IN THE DEMOCRACY AND TYRANNY PROGRAM

1. Monday and Wednesday meetings

These meetings included lectures, slide shows, debates, guest speakers, and dramatic presentations.

2. The Book Seminars

Ten to twelve students and a teacher made up a Seminar. Each Seminar met for three hours twice a week on assigned core books. The core books were:

- Frank J. Frost, *Greek Society*
- H. D. F. Kitto, *The Greeks*
- Homer, *The Odyssey*
- Aeschylus, *Oresteia*
- Aeschylus, *Prometheus Bound*
- Sophocles, *Oedipus the King*
- Sophocles, *Oedipus at Colonus*
- Sophocles, *Antigone*
- Xenophon, *Recollections of Socrates*
- Plato, *Eurhyphro, Apology, Crito*
- Plutarch, *Lives of the Noble Greeks*
- Sappho, *Lyrics*
- Pindar, *Odes*
- J. Broadman, *Greek Art*
- Thucydides, *The Peloponnesian War*
- Plato, *The Republic*
- Ben Shahn, *The Shape of Content*
- D. M. Potter, *People of Plenty*
- Saint-Exupery, *Night Flight*
- R. Ellison, *Invisible Man*
- W. Golding, *Lord of the Flies*
- Goethe, *Faust*
- H. D. Thoreau, *Walden*
- J. Tussman, *Obligation and the Body Politic*
- R. Carpenter, *The Esthetic Basis of Greek Art*
- J. Updike, *The Centaur*
- A. deTocqueville, *Democracy in America*

- S. Plath, *Ariel*
- M. Angelou, *I Know Why the Caged Bird Sings*
- R. Frost, *Poems*
- W. Whitman, *Leaves of Grass*
- J. W. Fulbright, *The Arrogance of Power*
- E. Bellamy, *Looking Backward*
- Lewis Mumford, *Sticks and Stones*

3. The Notebook

Every week the student turned in one entry for his or her Notebook. Each entry filled at least five pages of 8½ x 11 paper with normal margins. This came to a total of 120 pages.

4. Wednesday Film Series

The college film series was a required part of the program.

5. Individual or Group Projects

Each student did a project, a sequence of projects, or took one of the modules offered by the individual contract faculty.

6. Evaluations

Each student was required to write a formal self-evaluation at the end of each quarter and to be evaluated by a member of the faculty.

HEALTH: INDIVIDUAL AND COMMUNITY
Fall, Winter and Spring Quarters, 1977–78

Health: Individual and Community was an interdisciplinary program taught by four faculty with backgrounds in biology, ecology, psychology, and community planning. The primary goals of the program were the strengthening of basic learning skills (reading, writing in several contexts, critical thinking, and self-confidence in thought and communication) and the acquisition of knowledge that addressed the question *"What is a healthy state of being?"* Students were introduced to basic language, concepts, and research skills in the biological and social sciences, offered the opportunity to explore specific health topics in more depth, introduced to literary works with health as a metaphor or theme, and encouraged to examine their own lives to find ways of making the information and ideas of the program personally applicable.

The texts, *Biology: A Human Approach* (Sherman and Sherman), *Human Biology and Ecology* (Damon), *The Psychology of Women* (Williams), *Using Psychology* (Holland), *The Death and Life of Great American Cities* (Jacobs), and *Urban Health in America* (Ford), were the principal readings to accompany a series of lectures and labs given by the faculty the first half of fall and winter quarters and the first week of spring quarter. An exam concluded the fall and winter series. The following topics were included:

Fall:

>   Biology: Principles of structures and function of the cell, including cell metabolism and cell reproduction;
>   Ecology: Basic ecological concepts, including energy flow, succession and community structure;
>   Community Studies: An introduction to Ekistics: Warren's structure/function model, and change agents;
>   Psychology: Definition and basic principles of psychology: psychology of women; introduction to developmental psychology.

Winter:

>   Human Physiology: The major physiological systems (nervous, endocrine, cardiovascular, respiratory, renal and digestive);
>   Health Care Systems: Philosophies and practices in different cultures (primitive, China, Canada, Jamaica); health care planning and delivery in the U.S.

Spring:

>   Evolution: History of evolutionary thought; the genetic basis of change; cultural evolution; principles of sociobiology.

Each quarter students also chose one of two options for more in-depth study. These each required a research paper. The choices were:

Fall:

>   Animal Reproduction: *Reproductive Patterns* (Austin and Short), seminars and films were used to examine species differ-

ences, environmental effects, and behavior patterns on mammalian reproduction; written and oral library research reports;

Environment and Psychology: *Anthropopolis* (Doxiadis) and *The Cultural Experience* (Spradley and McCurdy) were used to look at the environment and special needs of individuals and groups in our society; ethnographic field research reports.

Winter:

Environmental Health: Materials from the center for Disease Control in Atlanta were used to learn the basic principles and techniques of epidemiology, including the use of statistics and graphics; case study problems and reports.

Brain and Behavior: *The Biological Basis of Mental Activity* (Hubbard) was used as the basis for discussions on the functional anatomy and physiology of the brain in both normal and abnormal states; written and oral library research reports.

Spring:

Political and Ethical Issues in Health Care: *Doing Better and Feeling Worse* (Knowles), student research, and seminars were used to explore issues such as technology, financing, medical education, and primary care; written research reports.

The Detective Novel: An Excercise in Logical Thinking: *Thinking Straight* (Beardsley) and five mystery novels were used to study theories and applications of logic; weekly problem sets.

Small seminar groups (8–10 students) met weekly to discuss literary works that used health as a metaphor or theme. Fall quarter, *Mirage of Health* (Dubos), *An Enemy of the People* (Ibsen), *Eden Express* (M. Vonnegut), *Cancer Ward* (Solzhenitsyn), and *The Plague* (Camus) were selected. Winter quarter's books were *Ishi in Two Worlds* (Kroeber), *Return to Laughter* (Bowen), *Mainstreet* (Lewis), and *The Jungle* (Sinclair). *Something Happened* (Heller), *Hillbilly Women* (Kahn), *Memoirs of a Dutiful Daughter* (de Beauvoir), and *The Golden Notebook* (Lessing) were read spring quarter. Students wrote essays to introduce and help focus the discussions.

Spring quarter, students devoted about half of their program work to group projects they had selected and planned. In a few cases students worked alone or pursued a part-time internship. The group projects were:

High Altitude Physiology: Studying the physiological changes which occur at altitude during acclimatization; 5-day trip to Mt. Ranier where actual changes were monitored and analyzed.

Stress: Studying the theory of Hans Selye and ways of assessing, relieving, and avoiding stress; planned stress "theme week."

Human Resources Planning: Studying social service planning, funding and delivery in Thurston County; producing a slide-tape show for public education.

Park Ecology: Studying the ecological food webs, the economic impacts on adjacent residential homes, and the social values of urban parks, particularly Sylvester Park in Olympia.

Nuclear Education: Studying the principles of nuclear power production, and the social, economic, and environmental impacts of nuclear plants; producing a slide-tape show for high school classes.

Anorexia: Exploring the historical, cultural, and medical influences on the thin fashion of contemporary women.

Low-level Radiation: Studying the effects of low-level radiation on humans; preparing a pamphlet for public distribution.

Students also kept a notebook of daily writings. Activities, ideas, or information generated by the program were explored, interrelated, and personalized. These notebooks were shared weekly with others in the seminar group. They became a personal history of the thinking and learning stimulated by the program.

Human Sexuality, Nutrition, and Stress were the topics of intensive "theme weeks" each quarter. Other components of the program included keeping a personal health assessment notebook and inviting health practitioners working in a wide variety of health careers to weekly informal luncheons.

SHAKESPEARE AND THE AGE OF ELIZABETH
Fall, Winter and Spring Quarters, 1978-79

Our overall program goals were for students to immerse them-selves in the sixteenth century; to learn to understand and enjoy the history and literature of the Elizabethan period with a special emphasis on Shakespeare; and to develop the appro-priate reading and writing and discussion skills. Fall quarter we moved fairly quickly in order to begin with an effect of immer-sion. We read a play each week for one seminar, a major prose work each week for the other seminar, and three or four back-ground works in addition.

All students were expected to read the following works:

— William Shakespeare: *Taming of the Shrew, A Midsummer Night's Dream, Much Ado About Nothing, Richard III, Richard II, Henry IV* parts 1 & 2, *Merchant of Venice, Twelfth Night,* "Venus and Adonis," "Phoenix and the Turtle," and "Lover's Complaint."
— Christopher Marlow: *Dr. Faustus*
— Ben Jonson: *Volpone*
— Baldesar Castiglione: *The Courtier*
— Niccolo Machiavelli: *The Prince*
— Erasmus: *The Praise of Folly*
— Thomas More: *Utopia*
— J. E. Neale: *Queen Elizabeth I*
— A. L. Rouse: *The Elizabethan Renaissance*
— E. M. W. Tillyard: *The Elizabethan World Picture*
— S. Shoenbaum: *William Shakespeare, A Documentary Life*
— C. S. Lewis: *Studies in Words* (sections)

Most of these readings were discussed in two weekly seminars. As part of seminar activities, all students were expected to write three papers: a short paper on a historical topic; a short paper on a literary topic; and a longer paper on the program theme question, Why was the Elizabethan period and/or Shakespeare so special?

Students were expected, in addition:

— to attend a weekly lecture on Shakespeare;
— to participate in informal readings of the play of the week in small groups;

— to see the following movies which were shown as part of the program: *A Midsummer Night's Dream, Elizabeth and Essex, Much Ado About Nothing, Edward II, Richard III, Chimes at Midnight, Henry V;*

— to write a letter of reflection at the end of the term about their learning over the quarter.

Finally, all students were expected to devote about a quarter of their program time to one of four writing workshops which met weekly and required weekly writing: grammar workshop (especially for students who wanted or needed to emphasize the essentials of correct writing); dream-reflection writing workshop; creative writing workshop; and history writing workshop. Winter quarter, as we concentrated on Shakespeare's middle period, and spring quarter, as we concentrated on his later plays, we somewhat slowed our pace, reading fewer plays more slowly and carefully. In particular we focused on *Measure for Measure* winter quarter and *The Tempest* spring quarter, using the scholarly Arden edition for each of them.

All students were expected to read the following works:

Winter Quarter:

— William Shakespeare, *Measure for Measure, Macbeth, Troilus and Cressida, Hamlet.*
— Philip Sidney, Selected poetry and "Defence of Poetry."
— Alfred Harbage, *Shakespeare's Audience.*
— A. L. Rowse, *The Elizabethan Renaissance.*
— G. Dickens, *The English Reformation.*
— O. Barfield, *Saving the Appearances.*
— A. Koyre, *From the Closed World to the Infinite Universe.*
— S. Shoenbaum, *William Shakespeare, A Documentary Life.*

Spring Quarter:

— William Shakespeare, *Othello, King Lear, Antony and Cleopatra, The Tempest, Henry VIII.*
— Thomas Middleton, *The Changeling.*
— Caroline Spurgeon, *Shakespeare's Imagery and What It Tells Us.*
— Montaigne, *Essays.*
— Robert Burton, *The Anatomy of Melancholy.*
— Loren Eisley, *The Man Who Saw Through Time.*

These readings were discussed in seminars held twice a week. As part of seminar activities, students were expected to write two or three short papers and a longer term paper. Students were expected in addition to attend weekly lectures (two per week, winter quarter).

Winter quarter students were expected to devote about a quarter of their academic efforts to work in one of four workshops: 1. Shakespeare's Sonnets; 2. Tudor Lives; 3. Writing Workshop; 4. Rewriting Workshop. Spring quarter, students were expected instead to do an independent project of their own choice.

At the end of winter quarter there was an all-day exam covering everything studied for fall and winter quarters.

3

PRIME DESIGN FEATURES

As I said earlier, my purpose in writing this report is to record what became of the Meiklejohn-Tussman-Cadwallader pedagogic model during its life at The Evergreen State College from 1970 to 1980. Obviously, a larger purpose is to make available to professors at other colleges a possibly interesting option for the refreshment of their work lives (and those of their students) who may then choose to add further chapters to the story. Although I considered it necessary, for purposes of basic communication, to include some illustrative descriptions of coordinated studies curricula, I harbor no illusions that having done so will achieve either purpose. Because, if we have proven anything in the experiment at Evergreen it is that, while ingenious curricular designs have come and gone, Meiklejohn's collaborative teaching idea has been a steady challenge, which continues to turn the threat of stagnation into the promise of renewal for a significant number of faculty and students.

Therefore, in the remainder of the report, I shall concentrate on what we have learned about the various structural features of the approach, and on the modifications of it that our experience has called upon us to make.

THE FACULTY TEAM

Teams of two to seven faculty members have staffed Evergreen's programs of coordinated study. Although it has been found that a program can be successful under all of these arrangements, four seems to be the optimal number. With less than four the holding of faculty seminars becomes awkward. This problem can be assuaged by inviting the participation of guest lecturers, or colleagues who are not then teaching in a team, but the qualities of intellectual comradeship are not the same as when the composition of the faculty seminar remains the same for the full year. With more than four, communication and logistic problems can strain the team's congeniality quotient.

The best programs have been those in which this sense of congeniality was strong prior to the program's conception, either on the basis of personal friendship or on the basis of mutual intellectual attraction. The broad curricular idea may have been hatched in passing during a faculty seminar of a previous program, and subsequently become the subject of playful brainstorming over lunch or beer. Other colleagues, getting wind of the thing, and being on the lookout for an enjoyable program in which to work the following year, begin to hover with questions and suggestions. The nucleus of a congenial faculty team has formed.

While the theme and broad outlines of a program may be the brainchildren of one person (who then usually becomes the program's coordinator), the fine tuning of the program – the choosing of books and films, the planning of lectures, seminars and workshops, weekly scheduling – must be the joint effort of all of the team's members. In no other way can the strengths of personal involvement and mutual commitment be assured which will inevitably be necessary to resolve unforeseeable differences.

Faculty with no previous experience in collaborative teaching must sometimes be recruited into a team, if the idea is to have a future. No more than one new recruit at a time is the rule I would suggest. The experienced faculty members at least know they are going to feel insecurities they didn't know they had –

every time around. The inexperienced faculty member, not being thus prepared, must be helped by the others to live through a period of professional and personal shock. Not the least of the frustrations, especially for an experienced teacher of courses, is the prescription against teaching his subject, in favor of learning how to *represent* it. Two other sources of shock are inevitable: (1) finding oneself totally responsible for the education of a group of students for a whole academic year, and (2) working under the constant scrutiny of professional peers. However sympathetic this scrutiny may be, it is trying on a beginner.

The planning faculty opted against faculty rank and tenure, in order to remove these as possible sources of tension within the faculty teams, so I cannot report on how teams might function which consisted of members of differing rank; much less of tenured and nontenured members. My guess is that such teams would find it impossible to develop the qualities of honesty and candor which effective team-teaching requires. On the other hand, I can think of no reason why a team in which all of the members were tenured might not learn how to enjoy each other, all other considerations being positive.

Tussman speaks of the importance of the program's "constitution," in which the members of the faculty team agree to subordinate their disciplinary expertise to the larger purpose of exploring the program's theme. In the Evergreen version this has evolved into the tradition of the program covenant. The covenant spells out in writing an agreed-upon procedure for resolving whatever disputes may later develop between the team members as to the program's philosophy, objectives, policies or practices. The pressures of collaborative teaching can become so intense, and the particular forms of conflict generated so unforeseeable, that we have found it useful to expect even the most personally congenial of teams to sign such a covenant before they meet their students. These have ranged from the extremely legalistic to the casual. One faculty team which, as it turned out, had good reason for expecting trouble, drew up a seven-page document of litigation procedures exemplified in a variety of scenarios. Another team simply resolved that in any given dispute the faculty member who felt the strongest about his position would carry the day – and it worked. The only situation worse than a team having to enforce its covenant is a team which does not have a covenant to enforce.

Most covenants also include assignments of administrative chores. Someone has to oversee the budget, someone has to order the books and films, someone has to be sure that film projectors and tape recorders are where they should be when they should be, someone has to make travel arrangements for retreats and field trips, someone has to make arrangements for seminar and lecture hall space, someone has to take responsibility for the program mailbox, etc. These menial but essential functions are more smoothly discharged if everyone knows from the beginning who is responsible for what.

From a pragmatic point of view, the question of how much of its time the faculty team should be able to commit to the program remains open. Meiklejohn's program could afford a commitment of two-thirds time; Tussman's could afford three-fourths; all of Evergreen's first programs committed their faculty teams to 100 percent. But one of the compromises we have had to make, for the sake of survival as a state institution, has been a steady decline in the number of programs to which we could afford to commit the full-time of faculty teams. Issues of institutional survival aside, from an educational point of view, I think a very definite finding of our first ten years has been that anything less than 100 percent faculty team involvement is a costly saving. It may eventually be discovered that a program of coordinated study in which the faculty team has other teaching commitments is a contradiction – like trying to save a marriage by having an affair.

THE PROGRAM THEME
(OR PROBLEM AND/OR PROJECT)

This coordinating thread should be one which is interesting in its own right, which cannot be adequately explored by any one discipline, and which invites exploration by all of the disciplines represented on the faculty team.

The program's theme should not be confused with its objectives. The objectives of the human development program were to learn how to read with discrimination, to write with style and to think with clarity – and to learn something of the social sciences and the humanities along the way. The coordinating theme was "the dialectic of overlapping generations," and its coordinating project was to write a psychohistorical study of one of one's parents. The objectives say what the students are supposed to learn. The theme seeks to insure that they will do this from a multidisciplinary point of view and with a sense of common purpose.

The theme may, initially, be incomprehensively complex (the dialectic of overlapping generations) or it may be disarmingly simple (What is a healthy state of being?). The project may be achievable (writing a psychohistorical study of a parent) or it may be one whose achievement is unlikely (writing a book which gets published). It does not seem to matter, from the points of view of encouraging interdisciplinary study and communion of purpose, so long as the faculty remember to keep the theme and/or project constantly at the forefront of everyone's consciousness. The lectures should refer to it often. A seminar should not be permitted to end without being asked to address its discussion to it. Every comment on every paper should refer to it. Multidisciplinary mindsets and habits of cooperative learning are foreign to American college students who, therefore, cannot be expected to embrace them overnight. Repeated demonstrations and reminders are necessary. Most Evergreen students go through at least the first quarter of their first program is if they were still taking separate courses in competition with their peers, with the familiar primary purpose being to try to please the teacher – despite there being no requirements, majors, or grades to remind them of these old habits.

The early signs of a program's success (usually coming in the second quarter) are when the students begin to try to pivot their responses to the books, and to each other's seminar contributions on the theme. And to try to help (rather than contend with) each other, because they have discovered that the thematic references unfold and build more enjoyably that way. By spring, if the faculty has been religious in its attention to the theme, it may be possible to give a lecture, such as one I once gave, on the nature of human language, which centered on *Moby Dick,* and which referred to works by Freud, Erikson, Shakespeare, Arthur Miller, Margaret Mead, Faulkner, Kafka, Joseph Heller and Alexis de Toqueville — knowing that the students would recognize, understand and enjoy the references, and knowing, too, that they themselves would address the lecture to the dialectic of overlapping generations in their seminars.

THE FACULTY SEMINAR

Although it has proven to be the most important feature of the experiment — at Berkeley and at Evergreen — the faculty seminar has also been the most readily misperceived and misused feature, and the most fragile one. It is readily misperceived because it runs counter to the traditional mores that tacitly govern the conduct of faculty scholarship: that it be original and that it be pursued independently of one's teaching. It is readily misused because of the ease with which the urgencies of business, bookkeeping and problems of governance can eclipse intellectual curiosities. It is fragile because it requires a high degree of personal courage, emotional stamina and integrity of character on the parts of all of its members to carry a faculty seminar from its days of survival into its days of usefulness and over into its self-perpetuating days of regularly anticipated pleasure.

At a faculty retreat, which was held after Evergreen's third year, in June 1974, during which much pain, frustration and exhaustion were expressed, a colleague who had been with us for two years, Leo Daugherty, wrote this about faculty seminars:

Lots of people are talking about curriculum, faculty burnout, "Is Coordinated Studies Worth All the Grief?" and a million other problems that somehow seem connected.
We live in a time when everything seems connected.
At least, all *problems* do.
While hopes and wishes and aspiration seem not to be, except as one more hope.

And we keep looking for an answer that will unify them and make them — make "it" — happen.

Rudy Martin suggested in the meetings that the Faculty Seminar is a good answer. I believe that. It has worked for me. And it has worked for just about everybody I know here who has really tried it. It isn't an all-purpose panacea. But it is also not merely a placebo that makes you feel better for no organic reason. It *is* organic. And it *is* good medicine, both curative and preventive. Mostly because it is fun.

So here are ten ideas I have about faculty Seminars:

1) *Hold* them. Once a week.

2) Make them your top priority in Coordinated Studies — the most important thing you do during your week.

3) A good idea is to make them public, with students and deans and the Provost and the President invited. The students in your program should not, probably, be "required" to come, or "strongly expected" to come, but just announce to them the time and place of your meeting. Once you get settled, however, lock the door and put a Do Not Disturb sign up. Communicate the idea that this is a very important thing to you, and that people should be on time or not come. In the two programs I've taught in, we experimented with the idea of "pretending that students aren't there." The faculty sit around a table, with students grouped in another area of the room, and with it being understood that they can't talk, even to ask questions at the end. That's because the Faculty Seminar is for *you,* not for them. Yet lots of them will want to be there, and they will like it. The alternative is to exclude them totally, but my experience has been that there's no reason to do this if the above rigidities are held to.

4) Make the Seminars about books or topics you're reading or thinking about together.

5) Do not do *any* program business at them.

6) Personal stuff (your nervous breakdown, divorce, etc.) should be kept to a minimum. (That kind of stuff is better dealt with over a beer or a cup of coffee off-campus, and it usually *must* be dealt with, and not avoided by you and your teammates. But the Faculty Seminar is something else.)

7) Make no overt attempt to have the Faculty Seminar feed into your teaching. It is for you. Both you and your teaching will be better for doing it this way.

8) Write position papers for them. One position paper per meeting is usually enough. They can be in the form of letters.

9) #2 and #8 seem to add up to your *taking all day* for the Faculty Seminar. Prepare in the morning (through reading or writing your position paper or writing a response to last week's meeting), have lunch, and meet in the afternoon. I've found Friday to be the best day to hold them. There are lots of reasons why, but the most important one is that it gives you something to really look forward to all week. (The objection is that, since it isn't a required function, your students might take a three-day weekend. But we've already given our students so much of our trust at Evergreen that this seems a trifling consideration. Just tell them you don't want them to take a three-day weekend (if you don't) and suggest some things they might do on Friday if they don't plan to attend. You'll have lots of ideas).

10) Memorialize them. Make tape recordings. Take extensive notes on what people say. Ask artistic students to make sketches. (Video-tape is a point of controversy here. It usually isn't very good. I have no idea why.)

P. S. It is tempting to talk about teaching problems in the Faculty Seminar. Different people will respond to that temptation in different ways. My own suggestion is to minimize such talk during the Fall Quarter meetings, while forcing yourself to really talk about books and issues, unless you have a teacher on your team who is new to Evergreen or new to teaching.

Daugherty chose well when he described the faculty seminar as *organic*. Somehow, they are made necessary by the confinements of teaching in a coordinated studies team, and they are also *made possible* by those same confinements. I have never experienced anything like them, and although I have known nine years of them, week after week, no words that come to me can adequately describe the experience; except, perhaps, the chancy metaphor that they are the satisfying sex of collaborative teaching which has its way of sustaining the family behind the scenes. For example, at the end of my first program at

Evergreen, in which we absolutely excluded students from even being spectators at the faculty seminars, we sent around a questionnaire which asked the students to rate those features of the program which had contributed most to whatever had done them the most good: lectures, seminars, books, films, workshops, etc. First in the ratings of the 120 students, by a wide margin, was the faculty seminar. Subsequent interviews revealed that the students had perceived the faculty seminars to be the weekly event which had enabled the faculty team to sustain its interest in serving them imaginatively, despite all of the miscalculations, mismanagements and oversights that had to have been part of the first year of the experiment.

Daugherty's enthusiasm for making the faculty seminar public needs some qualification. The experience to which he referred was with an especially amicable team, one that had previously worked very hard at having good faculty seminars by themselves, and had learned how to make them formal occasions for the concentrated exchange of ideas, despite the impossibility (in so intimately familiar a social setting) of performing roles. That team, and a few others like it, discovered that the pleasures to be had from meeting so unusual a challenge were enhanced when the temptations to perform roles were intensified by the presence of an audience. To successfully pretend that the students are not there when they are, requires an unusually demanding kind of virtuosity in the art of seminaring. Until the team has learned how to exchange ideas in ways other than performing them, however, it should hold the seminars in the privacy of someone's home, as Tussman did. The majority of Evergreen faculty seminars have been held in private.

Thus, faculty seminars may be compared to the jam sessions which groups of jazz musicians like to have after the audience for which they have performed has gone home. Free of the necessity to perform for the audience, and free of the possibility of doing so (with colleagues who know each other too well to permit mere performance) the time is ripe to just play for the hell of it. Some jazz groups then go on to have their jam sessions in public.

Traditional scholarly forums cannot pose such a challenge. In the faculty colloquia and symposia that I knew before coming to Evergreen, the test of how productive they were lay precisely in how well the participants performed their various roles. The institutional and interpersonal conditions were such that nothing but the performance of roles was possible. The participants were prevented by their daily jobs as teachers of courses from knowing each other's professional moves well enough to support scholarship for the hell of it. This may be how the term "academic" came to carry pejorative connotations in one of its usages. The faculty team of a coordinated studies program may or may not learn to have scholarly seminars, but it is impossible for it to have "academic" ones, in that sense.

The three prime design features of a program of coordinated study are those that I have just described: a congenial faculty team, a viable theme, problem or project, and satisfying faculty seminars. If these have been given top priority in the program design, and if they remain strong through the life of the program, nothing can go wrong in connection with any of the program's other features that cannot be made right. If any one of these three is overlooked in the designing of the program, or if any of them seriously deteriorates during the program's life, nothing else can prevent the program from either failing or becoming the equivalent of a set of courses.

This is a good time to enter my own judgment of the pedagogic form as a whole, as compared to its traditional equivalent: a set of separate courses. Tussman was unequivocal in his judgement.

> If the program were only as good as, or slightly better than, the present pattern of lower-division education, it would not be worth bothering with. It is not just a little better. It is infinitely better. (*Experiment at Berkeley,* p. 22.)

My experience, and that of scores of my colleagues at Evergreen, confirm Tussman in this. Participation in a successful program of coordinated study *is* infinitely better than enrollment in a set of separate courses. It is another order of educational experience altogether. It is neither something the faculty feel they have given, nor something the students feel they have taken. It is something both parties feel they have palpably lived together. It is a highly memorable experience, and, as such, much more of the learning that occurs in it is remembered than is notoriously the case in the taking of courses. Hundreds of Evergreen alumni, right now, I know, think back on some program in which they participated as one of the peak experiences of their lives. And while this may sometimes be said of the memory of some particular course, or some particular professor, I doubt that it has ever been said of the memory of a set of courses.

However, because our experience with the form has been longer and more varied than was Meiklejohn's or Tussman's, I can also state that participation in an *un*successful program of coordinated study is *infinitely worse* than enrollment in a set of separate courses. One's feeling of personal investment in a course is usually a measured one, whether you are a student or a teacher. If one or two turn out to have been a mistake, there are others in which you can compensate by increasing your investments in them. At worst, the memory is of having been unlucky. One's feeling of personal investment in a program of coordinated study is usually an *un*measured one, whether you are a student or a teacher. It is a go-for-broke situation all around. And, if *it* turns out to have been a mistake, no one feels merely unlucky. The teachers feel that they have utterly failed and the students feel that they have been betrayed.

As for the programs that neither succeed nor fail, they usually achieve this irresolute state by drifting into coursedom, and so there is not much to choose, in retrospect, between the chances you took when you enrolled in the program and the chances you would have taken had you taken (or given) a set of courses. However, the situations are not quite equivalent. At a traditional college, faculty members are expected to teach courses. Most of them, therefore, try to teach good courses, so as to take pride in their work. Many, as is well known, teach bad courses anyway, for a brace of other reasons. But to teach a good course is something in which a faculty member of a traditional college can take genuine professional pride. It is something to brag about. An Evergreen faculty member, on the other hand, who survives a poorly conceived or ineptly staffed program by way of teaching de facto good courses, may justifiably feel competent but he cannot feel proud. It is something to keep quiet about. And so, since professional pride is an important ingredient in the quality of college teaching, I would advise a child of mine to transfer to the university if I knew that the alternative were a coordinated studies program that was destined to devolve into a set of well-taught courses.

4

AUXILIARY DESIGN FEATURES

The auxiliary design features of a program of coordinated study are its book seminars, lectures, assemblies, workshops, examinations, conferences, retreats, business meetings, down days and evaluations. (I shall discuss evaluations in a separate chapter). All of these, excepting the retreats and down days, are familiar instructional devices, but in programs of coordinated study they are instructive for unfamiliar reasons and in unfamiliar ways.

BOOK SEMINARS

Most college professors would agree that seminars are superior to classes. Nevertheless, most undergraduate education in America takes place in classes. This reflects the degree to which academic departments are preoccupied with their majors and with preparing students for graduate work. The preoccupation inevitably puts a premium on "covering the materials," and classes are better than seminars for that purpose. The vast majority of college students are thus required to ingest large bodies of ultimately useless information by preparing for careers which they will not pursue. At the same time they are denied, without their knowledge, the opportunity of devoting their college years to learning how to do the more important things that need to be done to information by an educated adult: choosing and finding it, weighing it, criticizing it, analyzing it, comparing it, reflecting on it, editing it, and then expressing what has been made of it by way of spoken and written language.

By making book seminars the instructional centerpiece of a program, we turn the priorities diametrically around. Covering the book is not nearly as important as doing something interesting and meaningful with it. Helping the students convert this reversal of priorities into consonant changes in attitudes, expectations and study habits is the seminar leader's prevailing responsibility. In a first-year program consisting of high-school graduates it can take upwards of the whole year for most of the students to make this conversion. Until the conversion occurs, nothing else that goes on much matters.

It is exceedingly difficult for a professor with a doctorate in his subject whose intellectual tastes have perhaps been refined by a lifetime of cultured activities, to retain this conviction. But retain it he must, if the book seminar is to become anything but a class in disguise.

The students must learn that a seminar is not a place to prove that they have read the book; the need for such proof should be unthinkable. Not to have read the book that everyone agreed to read together is not only a breach of personal responsibility, it is a breach of social etiquette. The students must also experience the wastefulness of finishing the book in the hour before the seminar begins. They must learn that time must be planned for reflecting on the book, for organizing notes on it, for rereading parts of it and for writing something in response to it. This is why the booklist of most programs is short, compared to the combined book-lists of three or four traditional courses — so as to make it possible for the students to engineer this very difficult change in their reading habits. Moreover, the students must learn that great books are not things that you read *once*, that they are read with optimal satisfaction only when reading *means re*reading.

The students must also revise their expectations of the teacher. Students have typically learned to expect that after they have proven to the teacher that they have read a book the teacher will then tell them what the reading of it meant, or should have meant. The seminar leader must be careful to frustrate this expectation in all of its manifestations. Of course, if the book happens to be in the purview of the leader's expertise, it would be gauche of him not to share his more knowledgeable thoughts on it with the students; going on, perhaps, to get them to see that less informed thoughts, namely their's, may be equally interesting. More often, the book will be outside of the leader's field of expertise. This does not make the leader a "co-learner," as some Evergreen faculty have been pained to find out. Rather, it puts the leader in the role of *model* learner, and it is this role into which the leader of a seminar puts most of his energy and imagination. He may have read this particular book for the first time along with the students, but, unlike the students, he has read other books like it; has learned, in general, how to push a book around, how to question it and make it speak to his particular interests, how to talk and write back to it. He cannot insist that the students learn to derive meaning from their reading experiences in his idiosyncratic ways, but he can share those ways, and he can and should insist that they develop their own — and be prepared to wait until they do.

The students must learn to regard each other differently. In classes they were competitors for the teacher's attention and approval. What one's classmates were learning, and how they were learning it, was a matter of indifference. What a classmate said, being primarily beamed to the teacher, might, at most, be the object of fleeting interest. If a class goes well, it means the teacher did well; if it goes poorly, it means the teacher had an off-day. A seminar, on the other hand, is a communal venture. The students must learn to speak and listen to each other as intently as they speak and listen to the leader. They are not competing with each other for anything. They are there to help each other express what the book meant to the range of interests represented in the membership, and to learn to enjoy this process. Knowing what your fellow seminarians are learning, and how they are learning it, become matters of selfish concern when your responsibility is to contribute to the holding of a good book seminar. Individual hang-ups, pet peeves, characteristic biases, blind spots and overworked metaphors become opportunities for expressing intimacy and mutual understanding, instead of causing silently suffered irritation. Both the overly talkative student who learns to measure his remarks and to do more listening, and the shy silent student who finally manages to hold the floor for a full minute receive a quality of communal reward which is far more encouraging than anything a teacher could give. If a seminar goes well, everyone takes credit for it. If a seminar unravels into two hours of aimless chatter, everyone has to assume some of the responsibility for that dreary experience. The first sign that a program of coordinated study is on its way to success is when the comparing of notes over coffee shifts from how *I* am doing to how *my seminar* is doing.

To devote your primary attention in a seminar to this conversion process is a very difficult thing to pull off, especially when at heart you may really be more interested in the book than you are in the students learning how to talk about it. I would have found this an impossible responsibility to meet were it not for the faculty seminars. There is where I expect to get my personal intellectual kicks, and where I do get them regularly. Having had my say about the book with my peers, about whose thought processes and communication skills I may feel pleasure or pain but not responsibility, and having heard them have their's, I am less tempted to take the play away from the students in *their* seminar, in order to satisfy my own intellectual appetites. This is not the most important benefit to be gained from faculty seminars, but it is an important side effect.

Of course, individual professors will find their individual ways of meeting the responsibilities of seminar leadership, according to particular styles, temperaments, abilities and general interest in this sort of thing. My ways may work well for me, but I have seen colleagues, whose ways are the opposite of mine, lead beautiful seminars. However, there are three general objectives of which all seminar leaders should be mindful.

First, the students must come to believe that the qualities of thought, feeling and judgment with which they are reading the books, and the artfulness with which they are showing these qualities, are more important than the importance of the books.

If these skills are not being developed, it really does not much matter how important the books are that they are casting their eyes over. They will not hear you say this the first few times. When they hear it, they will not understand it for another few times. When they understand it, they will not believe it. When they believe it, they will not know how to act on the belief — and that is when you can stop the exhortations and, in your style, start the teaching, helping them learn how to act on the belief that reading an important book is only as important as one's abilities to think, talk and write about it.

Second, there is a very fine balance which book seminars should ideally achieve, although they rarely do, and the seminar leader is usually the only one who can be mindful of it. A book seminar has short-range and long-range objectives. In the short-range, the seminar should do justice to the book itself, and to the lecture, and to whatever other program activities may have centered on the book that week, and to what seems to be the members' general sense of attunement to the program theme on that day. In the long range, the seminar should do justice to itself. Each of its meetings should be a palpable growth experience in its life as a communal organism. Each meeting should ideally be, in other words, a satisfying end in itself and a means to future achievements of other satisfying ends. In an experienced seminar, the students can be expected to be mindful of both perspectives along with the leader. In a beginning group, it is the leader's lonely responsibility to do, or not do, whatever he can think of, intuit or guess, in order to balance the seminar's short and long-range needs.

Two examples will have to stand for the many: A brilliant and articulate student announces in an early seminar that he couldn't finish the assigned Margaret Mead book this week, because he became fascinated with the one for next month by Hannah Arendt, but this is all right, he says, because the Arendt book gave him some really interesting ideas on the program them, such as . . . The other members, happily surprised in being released from having to discuss the book they came prepared to discuss, start asking him questions about the Arendt book. His answers are interesting and informative ones. It sounds, and sort of feels like a good seminar. Only *I* know that if we don't get to discuss the Mead book, we'll resent having read it, and that if our potentially best student is rewarded for being a prima donna today, the seminar may not gain his full membership in the future. I compliment the student on his initiative and intelligence. I then remind him that the health of the program depends on everyone reading the same books at the same time, and discussing them on schedule; pointing out that he has so far prevented his friends from enjoying what they worked hard to be able to enjoy, and may even have jeopardized the seminar scheduled next month on Arendt's book. I add that references to books other than the one assigned are great if they are books we have all read, but that references to books that no one else in the seminar has yet read will probably be perceived as a counter-productive form of grandstanding. The seminar proceeds to make a stab at discussing the Mead book, but the discussion suffers from everyone mostly feeling sorry for the student and wondering what other kinds of strange outbursts they may expect from me. I have chosen to balance the long-range interests of the seminar as an *instrument* of learning against its short-range interests as an *instance* of learning.

A converse example is that of a young seminar which had been having a hard time following a consistent line of discourse. Most of the students had been working hard in preparation for the meetings and had resolutely been making thoughtful statements; but the statements are hovering over the table unrelated and having not much to say to each other. I ask if anyone sees the relevance of what has been said to the program theme. The question, being interpreted to mean that I think everything said so far was stupid and has *no* relevance to the theme, is met by stymied silence. The seminar has another hour to go and is on its way to disaster. I say, "If you don't mind, I'd like to give a short lecture." I proceed, in the next ten minutes, to show that from a particular point of view several of the statements made so far can be linked by a common conceptual thread, and that, when so linked, some interesting light can be cast on the program theme. Buoyed by this unexpected compliment, the seminar proceeds to a satisfying conclusion. In taking the play away from the students in this manner, I have set a risky precedent. A time will come when they will look to me for similar catalytic action when they are capable of providing it for themselves, and then I shall have to suffer the silence. For now, it didn't feel like play that I was taking away from them, and avoiding a painful failure today seemed to be important. I have chosen to balance the short-range interests of the seminar as an instance of learning against the long-range interests of the seminar as an instrument of learning.

Third, a book seminar can come to be regarded as something of a sacred ritual, suffused, at times, with a sense of reverence. Strange words to use in connection with modern education, I know. I take my cue from Suzanne Langer, who said: "Any man who loves his calling loves it for more than its use . . . entirely realistic performances may point beyond themselves, and acquire the value of suprapersonal acts, like rites." (*Philosophy in a New Key,* p. 243). In her discussion of rituals, Langer observes that they are highly mundane forms, charged, for the occasion, with powers of symbolic envisagement. Now, it doesn't happen very often, but it can happen that a seminar develops a quality of working esprit which makes it describable in such terms. It isn't articulated as such. No one says, "Hey gang, we're having sacred rituals here!" Rather, it takes the form of a growing sense that the seminar is accomplishing something more than is useful, that there is something symbolically meaningful going on, which points beyond schooling values, toward which reverence can be felt. Not reverence for the books, nor for the people in the seminar, nor for what they are accomplishing together – although these are all prerequisite. It is, I think, reverence for *this form of an occasion.* The form of a seminar – a small group of people, otherwise unrelated, who come together at a specified time and place to pursue a common interest – is, indeed, a mundane form, used for all sorts of useful purposes: committee meetings, classes, workshops, task forces, therapy groups and so on. The occasion of a satisfying book seminar, however, if repeated often enough, can symbolize something that may be archetypal in the literate human condition: that we are necessarily alone in respect to the culture in which we live, but that it is possible to express this aloneness to each other. To read a book is to confront one's culture in solitude. To join a seminar in which a group of others is reading the same books at the same time, for the purpose of sharing their solitary responses to them, is to be part of a very unusual occasion – one in which alonenesses can be made the ingredients of communality. Whether this explains why some seminars come to inspire reverence, I don't know. I only know that some seminars do come to regard their meetings this way, and that I cannot account for this by the mere fact that they are doing well in school together.

There isn't anything a seminar leader can do to encourage this development, other than to do everything else well (since it only happens in highly successful seminars), but it has helped me to stay mindful of the possibility.

LECTURES

In my first program of coordinated study we gave no lectures. Our previous teaching experience had led us to conclude that lectures were of little educational value, and we thought that an extra seminar would be a better way to occupy everyone's time. Subsequent experience revealed this to be an overreaction. Lectures are only of little educational value, I now realize, when teaching consists of little else than giving lectures. Composing and presenting three to five lectures a week cannot be an uplifting experience; and, therefore, cannot be received as such. Composing a good lecture is like making good bread: it can't be rushed. When lecturing is only a select part of the teaching, it need not be rushed.

The designs of most programs of coordinated study at Evergreen have called for one lecture a week. If the faculty team consists of four, each faculty member gets to do one lecture a month. At this pace, lectures become an entirely new experience – for all. The standards you find yourself trying to meet in composing and presenting your lectures tend to reflect the comfort that you have whole weeks in which to let them germinate, that the audience includes students and colleagues who are familiar with the ways in which your mind works and that the purpose of the lecture is to stimulate, rather than to replace, discussion. In these circumstances, lectures become occasions for scholarly self-indulgence, for doing justice to one's best thoughts about a book or a topic, without having to be concerned with student needs, which you know will be served in other ways.

There is also the knowledge that the audience has read the same books in the same sequence, and with the same thematic focus, so that you are in a position to amplify your thoughts by references to a familiar background of materials and interests. This makes for a quality of intimacy between lecturer and audience that I have not experienced elsewhere. A variety of adjectives might come to mind in seeking to describe the many lectures I have known at Evergreen; boring is not one of them.

Most lectures in the coordinated study format seek to relate the book of the week to the program theme by way of the lecturer's professional expertise. Inevitably, the lectures tend to build on each other as the year progresses, and to take on a serendipitous unity as a series. As the students come to perceive this unity, and to measure their growing abilities in interdisciplinary thinking against it, they come to appreciate the program, and their participation in it, with unusual satisfaction. The satisfaction of earning straight A's can't compare to it. Tussman says of this experience:

> One of the delights of the program is the growing sense of relation and interconnection as we progress. Each book seems to strike a note which reveals a new pattern or develops an old one. What we once read is always with us, and everything seems to get related to everything else. The unity of the program is the real context of each week, as the melody is the context of the note. (*Experiment at Berkeley*, p. 59.)

The ambience within which lectures in programs of coordinated study are experienced is also different. It is the only occasion of the week when all of the students and faculty come together in the same space. It is natural, therefore, for an all-program assembly to precede the lecture. The coordinator usually presides over the assembly. He usually has ten or fifteen minutes of announcements to make. The students usually have another ten or fifteen minutes of announcements to make (potlucks being organized, articles lost or found, films or plays coming up, car pooling, etc.). The mood is good-humored and casual. People are glad to see each other. Everyone is anticipating another stimulating lecture. Someone reading a poem or playing a piece of music signals the end of the announcements. The coordinator then introduces the lecturer who, of course, needs no introduction. There is applause. The lecture usually lasts for an hour to ninety minutes. A question period follows the lecture, until the coordinator calls the meeting to a close – more applause. This is not a setting in which it is easy to be dull.

A word about guest lecturers. They can, and do, add a dash of spice to the series, but they should not be scheduled during the early months of a program, for two reasons: (1) The students are eager to see *their* faculty in the lecturing situation. This has a way of settling whatever doubts may be lingering about having chosen to join the program. (2) A guest cannot addresss the lecture to the program theme, and to a sense of the students' appreciation of the theme; and it is very important to make frequent references to these in the first months. After the Christmas break is a good time to start occasionally bringing in some well-chosen guests.

WORKSHOPS

Not everything that needs to be learned in a program can be learned in book seminars. Book seminars are for learning how to let books affect our lives. The books should, therefore, be ones in which important questions, or positions of value or choice, are embedded. Books which merely contain useful information, and books which tell how to develop useful skills, do not lend themselves to being good subjects of seminars. Everyone should read the books on the program's reading list at the same time. Not everyone needs to acquire the same bodies of information, nor does everyone need to develop the same skills, at the same time. Thus, workshops.

The categories of information, and the types of skills, for which workshops should be designed will vary from program to program, of course. One program will need to teach some population genetics, another will need to teach something about interviewing techniques, another will need to teach some facts of Tudor history, another will need to introduce New Criticism, another will need to read Huizinga's *The Waning of the Middle Ages.* Not much needs to be said about workshops here. They are little classes, taught, as elsewhere, by way of reading, recitation, drills, exercises and tests, except that here they are adjunctive to a unified program of study. The best thing about doing workshops in this programmatic format is that students can often lead them.

There is one skill on which all college students, at all levels, need to work, and in which all programs should therefore provide workshops: writing. The Evergreen experience in teaching writing has been prolific. The approach with which I am most familiar is as follows:

1. The seminars are given a writing assignment. Say, a three-page paper relating *Catch-22,* or *Heart of Darkness,* to the program theme. The students are told that everyone in each seminar will read the papers of everyone else in their seminar.

2. The papers are written and handed in.

3. At the next assembly, the coordinator announces that the program will shut down for two days for a special exercise.

4. On the first day the seminars meet all day. Everyone reads everyone else's paper, and writes a one-paragraph precis of it. Everyone also copies down, on a separate sheet, those sentences from each paper which were unusually effective or enjoyable. We have come to call these the "irresistible" lines.

5. On the second day the seminars meet all day again. Each member reads his precis and irresistible lines on each paper out loud and the seminar discusses these in turn.

6. Each author then collects his set of fifteen or so editorial responses, for use in rewriting the paper.

7. The rewritten papers are made available to everyone in the Common Room.

I have then found it useful to capitalize on the students' discoveries of the joys of rewriting by offering a weekly Rewriting Workshop:

1. Each week two student papers are xeroxed and distributed to the seminar.

2. Everyone reads and makes written comments on the paper on the night before the workshop.

3. In the workshop we work as a group for about two hours on each paper, trying to agree on how it might best be rewritten. We go over every paragraph, sometimes every line, making concrete suggestions as to the paper's organization, grammatical correctness and style.

The authors then rewrite their papers and make them available in the Common Room.

These procedures have taught me why writing critical comments on student papers is almost always futile. All this does is prove to the student that you have read his paper. This information cannot help the student learn to write, because it cannot be used. It is like collecting intelligence after the war is over. The things that were wrong with the paper were wrong with *that* paper, not some other one; and the understandings of the English Grapholect which can make them right are most likely to come in rewriting *that* paper — not some *other* one. Critical comments on a paper only call attention to mistakes. The rewriting suggestions that are received from one's teacher and peers (all of whom are obviously learning to improve their own writing by helping you to improve yours) call attention to the mistakes *and to their possible corrections.* It turns the notoriously painful process of working on writing into a pleasure.

When I was planning my first Rewriting Workshop, I predicted it would be a glum experience. To my surprise, the students loved it. No one missed a session. Everyone's writing improved dramatically. Many said it was the most enjoyable feature of the program. From which I have had to draw the conclusion that students care more about leaning to write well than about anything else they can learn in college. That this is one of the best-kept secrets of college life must mean that the time-honored, isolated, critical comment approach drives this care underground. Who wants to admit wanting to do what seems impossible? Nothing has been more gratifying in my Evergreen experience than to learn how urgently students want to learn to write well, how quickly they can be helped to do so and how grateful they are for the help. Here are some excerpts from the evaluative comments on that first Rewriting Workshop:

Dear Richard,

Last night I went to a showing of first-effort films and video-tapes here at Evergreen. I saw a lot of drawn-out, boring movies. As I watched, I wondered what sort of concrete suggestions the faculty for that program would give them to help make their next efforts more interesting and watchable. Making a movie is a lot like writing, and these coming filmmakers would gain a lot from what we've been learning about rewriting.

The writing instruction I have received in the Shakespeare program is the best I have ever received. For the first time, I actually know how to make my writing better — write more and share it with others on whom I can count to tell me what they see. I know that putting an idea to paper, and having others understand and enjoy it, are what I am trying to do. For the first time, that process doesn't seem hopelessly difficult. The study of my and others' papers in the Rewrite Workshop brings writing from a solitary, frustrating struggle to a caring exchange of aid and assistance.

You aided me tremendously in your short workshop ramblings on writing "therapeutics." I have scribbled on top of one of my papers: "Motivation? Attitude? Concept of self? Audience?" These words, along with "What? So What? and Now What?" will always be in my bag of tricks. The writer's state of mind is so goddamned important yet so seldom mentioned.

The biggest single thing I learned is that I need to step out of myself, and use my ear (or eye) to judge how others receive my work. What seems perfectly clear to me in my writing may actually be confused or obscured to my reader. Hence, the need for a structure in my writing. Often, a paper I had thought had structure turned out to be loose or rambling, when read by someone else.

The Rewrite Workshop was worth more to me than years of teacher comments on papers.

Your student in Shakespeare,

Richard F. Jones

Dear Richard,

As I was reading Strunk and White — cover to cover — I thought, "I'll never remember this stuff!" While writing seminar papers, I was amazed at the number of rules I remembered and could apply to my writing. Reading the rewriting papers prompted still more recollection, and going over sentences line by line reinforced that recollection.

Going over the structure first, then going over the sentences, line by line, was exciting. It was a concrete formula for me to attack my own papers that were in need of rewriting. I didn't have a way to start, and then I did.

I was never bored with rewriting class. Every paper had a new problem that I have had at one time or another.

Richard, I would not change anything about the workshop. The method we all worked out worked perfectly for me. Reading Strunk and White cover to cover was an excellent idea. Pouring over the papers together in class; equally excellent. I developed my critical eye, my sentence structure, my punctuation and my organization. And of course, now, I rewrite seriously!

Sincerely,

Mary Young

To: Richard Jones
From: Susan Dimitroff
Re: Comments on the Rewrite Workshop

Dear Richard:

I think the Rewrite Workshop was a tremendous success. It was so helpful to present a paper and to get immediate feedback from friends. I liked hearing all the different ideas, and then having the option to pick and choose those ideas I wanted to keep and those I needed to discard or rewrite. The workshop gave me a useful and constructive awareness of my strengths (good organization and good use of language) and weaknesses (weak overall structure and confusing, complex sentences). I am now using this knowledge to write better papers. I also learned that the conclusion I reach in my rough draft may suggest the central structure of the final paper, and can often be used to germinate the opening paragraph of the final paper. I now look very carefully at my rough draft conclusion before writing the final draft. What a saving in time and frustration.

The paragraph by paragraph, sentence by sentence discussions were as valuable as the overall structure discussions. I needed to hear other students' ideas on all the papers. They enriched my perceptions of the different meanings of a sentence by suggesting subtle changes in structure and wording — changes I didn't think of and wouldn't have thought of.

I didn't care if a student needed help with fundamental writing skills rather than with rewriting. I felt it was most important that students who wanted to improve their writing skills were given the opportunity to do so.

I wish more people had had the time to rewrite their papers. It is quite an experience! I wrote the sonnet dedication paper after my workshop rewrite and I think it's the best paper I've written this year. It is so reassuring to *know* what to look for in a good paper and to know how to go about writing one.

This approach to teaching writing is, admittedly, time-consuming but it works. Students in large numbers do learn to write well. And I'd rather spend four hours with them, discussing rewriting strategies that pay off, than two hours by myself writing critical comments which will probably hurt more than they will help.

Actually, the Rewriting Workshop, as a title, is misleading. It is a *writing* workshop, the best kind, because, as most good writers learn early on, the art of writing only comes in efforts to *re*write.

The other thing I learned from this approach to teaching writing was that, while students will write anything to the teacher, to get it over with, they try their very best to get their writing started well when they know they are also writing to friends from whom they know they will hear.

EXAMINATIONS

Freed from having to support a competitive grading system, an occasional examination can be a very useful feature in a program. The students are usually enjoying the lectures and seminars, and are feeling good about their progress in reading, writing and talking; but many of them come to feel vaguely haunted by the suspicion that they may not be learning much of anything that is substantive. A timely examination is an effective way of inviting the students to dispel this doubt. I like to announce, in the first program syllabus, that a four-hour comprehensive examination will be given during the last week of the fall quarter, that sample questions will be given out well in advance, that the exam will not be graded but will be commented on and discussed in seminar, and that its purpose is to indicate what they have learned by that date and what they will by then need to review.

Approached in this way, the examination not only achieves its main purpose but several others as well. As the day approaches, and typical jitters begin to mount, the students begin to engage in the kinds of concerted, boning-up study in which they became specialists in high school. This kind of studying, many of them learn, is not only compatible with the more relaxed and thoughtful ways to which the program has introduced them; it can actually enhance those ways. There is nothing wrong, it dawns, with learning being a grind *some* of the time; only when it has to be a grind *all* of the time.

A week or two before the big day, students begin to form into small cliques for skull sessions, in which they pour over the sample questions and compare notes on possible answers. The day of the exam becomes almost festive. Most everyone is feeling reasonably confident; no one can be competing with anyone else, and, by this time, it has become clear to most that there can really be only one point in going through with it: to verify that a lot of substantive stuff has in fact been learned. In these conditions, almost all of the students report enjoying the experience, and they tend to remember the examination as a major event in the life of the program. The seminar leader may read and comment on the answers, but the primary "correcting" of the exams takes place in a subsequent seminar, where different kinds of right answers can be compared and discussed.

CONFERENCES

These serve the same purposes in a program of coordinated study that they do in a professor's ordinary office hours: personal counseling, academic guidance, discipline and tutorial reading-writing. However, there are curious counterbalances, as regard conferences, which develop in a program. On the one hand, the students actually need little conference time from the faculty, because many of the students can and do provide these services for each other. On the other hand, the students feel so close to their program faculty that many of them come to see an open office door as an invitation to have a chat about anything that happens to seem vaguely problematic at the time. Different faculty deal with this incongruity of program life according to different tastes. I happen to enjoy students only when I'm working for them, and so I schedule one office hour after each seminar and workshop which must suffice. If one student shows up, he can have the whole hour; if six show up, they can have ten minutes each. Moreover, I have learned that anything I can do for a student in a conference, I can do better in his seminar or workshop (excepting help with personal problems), because, there, he gets to see that solving his problem has also helped others solve their's. Consequently, I find myself giving less time to conferences in Evergreen programs than I did when teaching courses at Brandeis and Harvard. Many Evergreen faculty have chosen not to make this saving, and that's all right, too.

RETREATS

These are special occasions when the whole program goes off campus, for a few days to a week, to some idyllic place close to nature (there, are, fortunately, many of these left in the State of Washington) away from telephones, televisions, concrete buildings and power mowers, to do what we would otherwise be doing on campus.

I like to take the program on such a retreat in the third week. We have gotten into the routine, and it is beginning to feel routine. We lighten the schedule some, but we still do some reading and writing, hear a lecture and have a book seminar. Otherwise, there is nothing to do but get to know each other: taking hikes, cooking meals, playing cards, sharing anxieties, singing, dancing, and getting there and back. We show ourselves to be the particular persons we are, while remaining students and teachers. The program coheres in a thousand intermeshing ways which no professional "community builder" could devise. We have simply arranged a way to meet our responsibilities while having a good time. The chemistry for blending and reblending this meeting of responsibilities with pleasure tends to cook through the year.

Some programs have found a year-end retreat to be an enjoyable context within which to write evaluations. The evaluations tend to be taken more seriously, and are written with more candor, when everyone is doing them together in pleasant surroundings.

The possibility of holding retreats is a significant benefit of full-time programs.

BUSINESS MEETINGS

These are like little department meetings, except that a congenial team needn't give more than half an hour a week to them. Lunch at a local restaurant after the lecture is a pleasant way of doing the week's business, and catching up on college gossip. Business matters should never intrude on faculty seminars.

THE DOWN DAY

These are too tacitly assumed to be frequent in traditional settings to be in need of a name, but it is essential that a program's faculty be allowed one undisturbed day a week in their offices; for reading, writing, reflecting, composing lectures, planning seminars, etc. Some evenings and weekends are also absorbed in these activities; the purpose of the down day is to insure that *all* of them will not be. If the faculty settles on the same day as their down day, and the students know from the start what that day is, individual routines soon adjust and exceptions are infrequent.

A typical faculty schedule, then, looks something like this:

	A.M.	P.M.
Monday	Assembly-Lecture	Book Seminar
Tuesday	Workshop	Workshop
Wednesday	D O W N D A Y	
Thursday	Book Seminar	Conferences
Friday	F A C U L T Y S E M I N A R	

5

EVALUATION

The most significant improvement that Evergreen has made on the Berkeley and Wisconsin models has been in the area of evaluation. At Berkeley, Tussman had to reach what must have been an unsatisfactory compromise with the University's grading system. He described this as follows:

> After much uncertainty, the grade situation has been clarified. We did not – could not, since legislation was necessary – announce "pass-not pass" grading as a feature of the program. It quickly became apparent that adoption of such a system was highly desirable, and we deferred grading until legislative action by the Berkeley Division made adoption of the "pass-not pass" system possible. The student is given an option. He can indicate at the beginning of the semester, whether he wishes to be graded on the "pass-not pass" or on the conventional letter grade system. During the first year all but a handful chose "pass-not pass." We will be interested to see whether this changes. (*Experiment at Berkeley,* p. 98.)

Evergreen's planning faculty committed the college to a system of evaluation by portfolio, at all levels: student, faculty, and program. Students keep a portfolio, which includes samples of their best work, narrative self-evaluations, narrative evaluations by faculty and narrative evaluations of faculty. Faculty keep a portfolio which includes records of their teaching, scholarship and college service, narrative self-evaluations, narrative evaluations by students and colleagues and narrative evaluations of students and colleagues. The college keeps a portfolio of program histories, written by the faculty team at the close of each program.

No program description could convey what I meant when I said earlier that the Evergreen continuation of the Meiklejohn-Tussman model has revealed a whole new conception of what it can mean to go to college and what it can mean to teach in a college. If anything short of first-hand experience in a program of coordinated study can convey this, it is the tone and voice of Evergreen's evaluations. Therefore, I shall quote at length from a booklet on the Evergreen evaluation system, which I wrote for my collegues last year:*

LETTERS OF REFLECTION

As the end of the first quarter of a program approaches, most everyone feels the need for some kind of evaluation procedure to clear the air of uncertainties. This is not the time for formally evaluating the students' achievements, as many of these have yet to occur. Rather, exchanging candid letters of reflection at this part way point can go a long way toward insuring that optimal achievements will occur. Here is one that did:

---

*In this, I follow the example of Meiklejohn, who in seeking to convey the essence of his social invention, concluded that: "After all, the essential matter is that of the personal relation between the teacher and the pupil and of the mutual influences which pass between them." (*The Experimental College,* p. 172.) An interesting observation on the lengths to which the Evergreen system of evaluation has gone beyond that of its grandparent — and on the differences between the intergenerational dealings which were possible in the 1920s and in the 1970s, respectively — may be had in reading pages 172 to 210 of *The Experimental College,* which consists of a sample of the Wisconsin experiment's evaluations.

January 26, 1978

Karen K.

Human Development

Dear Karen,

Do you know that you are the only student in the Human Development program who has met *every requirement,* completed *every* assignment (including the dream diary) and done so *promptly, thoroughly* and *neatly?* Now *that* is pretty extreme behavior; as such, it invites both evaluation and interpretation.

My evaluation is that it is just fine. It says that you will probably never have to work at developing good work and study habits. People who do have to work at these (there are more than a few of them among your present colleagues) find it increasingly difficult to successfully do so as time passes. And it can become downright tragic for an intelligent adult, who has learned to think his or her own thoughts, to have to realize that they haven't learned the disciplines which enable the expression and sharing of those thoughts. You need never fear such a tragedy. You developed those disciplines long ago. You can just plain confidently take them for granted, forever and ever. You couldn't lose them if you tried.

Interpretation of this extreme behavior of yours is more of a challenge. There are probably several interpretations that would make sense. I shall concentrate on one: I'll speculate that it is part of a "get by" or "play it safe" syndrome, which can take over even when you genuinely want to do more than get by or play it safe. This tendency for it to take over, despite your more adventurous intentions, is probably the other side of your not having to worry about losing your discipline as a good student: they are so very much a part of you that they can and will take you over anytime you let them. Anytime you fail to represent your own distinctive thoughts, or choose not to, they will automatically take over, and say, in effect, "here, I'll say it in a way that at least won't displease."

Now, if this interpretation is valid, it is clear what you must learn to do: you must learn to make your discipline, skills, and habits *serve you*, and not allow yourself (*your* objectives, *your* purposes, *your* goals) to serve them. Will this involve you in becoming thoughtless, lazy or sloppy? No, those things you will forever find it impossible to be. What this *will* involve you in, and I shall put it in the form of a formula, is *taking chances with the powers of particularity.*

What do I mean by this? I think you sense it when you refer to your "highschoolish tendencies" and your "sense of duty" in your self-evaluation. And, as I said in my letter to the scholarship people, there are signs in some of your writings that you are making progress in the correction of those tendencies. But in your attempts, so far, you have merely been fighting the devil; you must also learn to *play* the devil. (Do you see what I just did, Karen? The risk I took? I know I'm on sensitive ground here, and I also know that you could completely misunderstand what I just said about playing the devil, because it isn't something a teacher will often recommend to a student. But I chose to take the risk, because when I'm writing I'd rather be misunderstood than not understood — which is what I'm encouraging you to do.) Which is what I mean by taking chances with the powers of particularity.

Let's look at some places in your self-evaluation where you (or "they") chose not to take such chances:

You say that Human Development represented a challenge. Well, if that is *all* you're going to say, you may as well not say it. I already know that. What I don't know, and only you can tell me (if you'll risk being particular) is *what* challenge the program represented *to you*. What was threatened *in you*? What was invited *from you*? Hell, the program represents a challenge to me, too. Maybe, if you showed me yours, I might show you mine. (You see how readily particularities can lead us into temptation! Risky, risky.)

You say the challenge to comprehend was a struggle, but the benefits from understanding were immeasureable. Well, now, you really are beginning to frustrate me, because if ever there was a particular benefit that I'd really like to think about, it would be an immeasurable one. But you don't let me in on

the particular understanding that carried that distinctive benefit. Not only don't you let me in on this, you positively with-
hold it from me. Frustrating. What was the struggle a struggle
between? How did it feel? Is it still going on? And so forth.

Studying the works of Freud and Erikson, you say, opened up
a new area of "thought and practice." Now you have really
done it! You have gone so far as to itch my imagination, and
given me nothing with which to scratch it. The new areas of
thought that studying Freud and Erikson tend to open, I know
a lot about. But new areas of *practice*? (To what could she be
referring? A new way of jogging, perhaps?) Oh, to be on the
threshold of knowing how Freud has influenced the *practices*
of a lovely young woman in 1978, and to see such knowledge
disappear, as her "enthusiasm and exhilaration were magnified
by eventual comprehension." Oh, I must say to you, lady,
that fighting this devil of unparticularity is too much for me.
I cannot go on.

So, I'll skip to the last paragraph — where (sigh) I find you
resolving to strive to achieve a sense of mastery over your
weaknesses. No, for God's sake! No, no, no, no. It is your
strengths over which you must strive to achieve a sense of
mastery. Your weaknesses, poor things, must be cultivated
and nourished. They are not yet strong enough to be mastered.
Feed 'em on particularities, and let 'em play with the devil. This
is the prescription you get from Dr. Jones, here at mid-year.
Try one particularity per paper; then two, and level off at
three for the rest of the year. Give goodness and truth a vaca-
tion, and try to stick to the sticky particularities of everyday
thought — yours.

Specifically yours,

Richard

In writing letters of reflection, when you are less interested
in what the student has so far achieved than in the particular
process of achievement (or nonachievement) that is mounting,
and in the part being played in that process by the relationship
that has been forming between you and the student, the

primary objective is *to challenge*. Nothing is more discouraging to a student at this part-way point in a program than to receive a dutiful in-house evaluation, addressed to some unknown third person, droning on about the student's "strengths" and "weaknesses"; and ending with a vapid pat on the back or slap on the wrist, as the case may be. In either case, the student senses that some kind of brush-off has happened, that the same statement could have been made (and may have been) about a whole category of students.

By comparison, nothing can be more encouraging to a student at this juncture than to receive a candid, well-written, detailed, eye-to-eye challenge to do better — *much* better — than she or he has been doing. The challenge should be such that it could clearly not be made to any other student on earth. The more strongly worded the challenge, the better. So long as you can say it with a smile. Put that down as the first rule of letter of reflection writing: *anything you say will ultimately be encouraging if you say it with a smile.* Here's one in which I succeeded in following that rule by the space of a hair:

January 30, 1978

Steve A.
Human Development

Dear Steve,

The first time you called me Dr. Jones, last summer when we were negotiating your contract, I felt like looking around to see if anyone else was in the office with us. Gradually, I became reacquainted with myself in those sounds. Eventually, I came to look forward to our weekly appointments, not only because you were doing such good work but because I knew I was going to feel the nostalgic satisfaction of recognizing myself in the words Dr. Jones.

When you decided to switch from the contract to the Human Development program, I knew that Dr. Jones' days were numbered. I also knew it would take some doing for you to reorient your transference from Dr. Jones to Richard. Which it did, remember? How long was it before "Dr. Jo ... uh ... Richard" was replaced by a comfortable "Richard?" About three weeks, wasn't it?

In retrospect, that is a very puzzling observation, because, in retrospect, something else was replaced around that time: Steve A., the serious; purposeful; hard-working; productive (if somewhat tight and overly self-effacing) student of the contract, by Steve A., the less serious; less purposeful; less disciplined; less productive (if more relaxed and more confident) student of the Human Development program. To me, this has been a puzzling development, and I want to devote this letter of reflection to the prospect of the two of us puzzling it into a mutually satisfying redevelopment.

The fact of the matter is that your take-home exam, submitted October 24, 1977, was the last piece of written work that matched the academic quality of the work you did in the contract. Why? I can't be sure, but I think it may partially stem from the influence that the seminars have had on your outlook on education. That's just a strong hunch. Seminars tend to encourage youngsters who are fresh out of high school to take their thoughts more seriously. Is it possible that after so many years of educating yourself, seminars have had the opposite effect on you?

I hasten to say that I have not for a second questioned the wisdom of your switching from the contract to the program. You are getting an immeasurably richer education in the program than you would have in our weekly meetings, interspersed by isolated readings and writings. Your participation in the program has, as you have said on several occasions, changed your life. I take this to mean that you are discovering that new thoughts and ideas can have enriching influences on your personal, social and emotional life as well as on your intellectual life. In the process, however, I wonder if you haven't allowed the motives and discipline that used to serve that box in your head, labeled "school," to wear thin.

I hope these speculations are on the money, because, if they are, then this let-up in academic commitment of the past two months can be seen as transitional in nature; as part of an holistic process of reorienting your life to a new approach to learning; of discovering, perhaps, that it can be as enjoyable as it can be useful — but no less purposeful and demanding for that. In other words, what we may have here is an interesting problem of integration.

How to start solving this problem? One way to start not solving it would be to simply resolve to work harder and to bear down. That won't do it, Steve. That would be a superego solution, and we're looking for an ego solution. Which means we're looking for a welcome surprise, for an a-ha experience of some kind. I suggest you start looking for this experience in the seminars. I'll be blunt: so far, in the seminar, you talk too much, and say too little.

A seminar, at its best (and, from week to week, we can only try for the best) is a time and place for *seminal* thinking. Seminal thinking can't come from the top of the head. It comes from considering what has been said, and then considering whether one's response is relevant to what has been said and then deciding whether what you are about to say expresses that relevance.

Am I saying that a seminar has to be somber and sour-pussed? Far from it. Only that humor should come from the conjoinment of ideas, and not at the expense of having the ideas.

For example, your joke about Gregor's "apple-ectomy," had it been better timed, would have been hilariously funny, and we could all have enjoyed it. As it was, it interrupted David's efforts to articulate a layer of meaning in the story that he had been waiting to share, and set the whole seminar back a step as a consequence. It was like someone cracking their knuckles during sex.

For example, since we had all agreed from the outset that *Metamorphosis* is anything (maybe everything) but a story about a bug, what was the point of your effort to bring entymological observations into the discussion?

If these critical observations have the effect of discouraging you, I shall be sorry. My purpose is to encourage you. To see that seminaring is an art, and must be approached as such. I really think this has not occurred to you, and the whole point of this letter is to help it to occur to you. (I'll have some more specific suggestions when we talk.)

For, my hunch is, once you begin to develop the art of semi-naring, the integration I spoke of earlier will have begun. And I shall be able to include you among Evergreen's more notable success stories.

Countering the transference,

Richard

" . . . like someone cracking their knuckles during sex." Should I have said that? I debated editing it out, lest it land below the belt. I decided to risk it — for three reasons: (1) I was sure I meant to help, not hurt. (2) The metaphor had never been inspired by the seminar participation of any student I'd ever worked with, so, whatever else it might say to him, it would also say that I was trying to think of him as the unique individual he is. (3) When the image came to me, it came with *a smile.*

Steve didn't enjoy receiving the letter. Our subsequent conference was tense. But he took it, as we used to say, like a man; and, later, after his seminar skills had improved, he thanked me for it.

This writing of challenging letters of reflection, must, of course, be custom-fitted to the capacities and sensitivities of the individual student. Lately, I find myself coming on like Jahweh with the stronger ones, and like your friendly Irish priest with the weaker ones. For example, to our very best student in Human Development, last winter, I wrote:

January 31, 1978

Matthew J.
Human Development

Dear Matt,

I have just re-read all of your writings (including, for the first time, your dream writings, which are consistently delightful) and have easily concluded that you are our seminar's ace student. Everything you say in your self-evaluation deserves to be said, and is, with a few exceptions (most notably the first sentence) well said. The trouble is, you and I are the only ones who know this.

How so, trouble? On two counts, both of which you intuitively anticipated in that memorable line of your writing on *Heart of Darkness* and Teresa's dream: "Differences demand attention!" As you say, your pen is mightier than your voice, and, as you imply, that difference has not had the attention it demands. You refer to this comparative weakness in your self-evaluation as "damaging." My first reaction was to see this as an over-statement. As I thought it through, however, I decided the word was well chosen. Yes, if you don't find a way for the develop-ment of your speaking voice to catch up with the development of your writing voice, damage may ensue.

First, it could damage the seminar. What good is it for a seminar to have an ace if it doesn't know that it has an ace? Indeed, what good is it to be an ace all by one's self? As a sage said: "What it's all about is not what it's all about. What it's all about is that we're all in it together." From the truth of which ultimately derives, I think, the power of the seminar as an educational device. Anyway, there you sit, week after week, with all those good "memorialized" thoughts that you have lately been learning to think, acting as if they could have no connection with what is being said, when in your heart you must know better. The next time somebody complains about the seminar being disconnected I may just say: "Blame our star student, Matt, the son of Jacob. He's got the connections (Isn't it with all twelve tribes of Israel?) and he's holding out on us." Putting it baldly, Matt, it's a matter of cheating, of not accepting your earned responsibilities. I mean, what do you want for being our ace student? An A? Not here, friend. All you get here, for having good thoughts, is more oppor-tunity to be a better friend. Kapish?

Secondly, if you fail to make good on the resolution with which you conclude your self-evaluation, the wind may go out of your writing voice. One's speaking voice is always differ-ent from one's writing voice, and *it is* a difference that demands attention, right. Effective writing improves one's clarity of speech. Effective speaking improves the clarity of one's writing. Good thinking issues from this on-going process of mutual improvement.

For example, I agree with you that the quality of your thinking and writing has been mounting at an impressive rate all year long, but there are still occasions when you embarrass both of us with sentences like the one with which you began your self-evaluation. Re-read it. That, Matt, is a piss-poor sentence. That you managed to rescue the self-evaluation from it, and went on to compose a pretty good document in spite of it, is almost miraculous. Dave Marr could tell you what is wrong with it — something in its predication, I think. What I know is that you would never, ever, even if drunk, *say* that sentence: "With psychology as my primary interest since high school, I had had some experience with. . ." No, you couldn't and wouldn't speak it. The point is that if you had been speaking your thoughts more, you probably wouldn't have written it. Your speaker's ear would have edited it into English, whether or not you knew anything about correct predication.

All of the above, I trust you understand, is meant to strengthen the courage of your own written (not yet spoken) commitment to round out your very considerable scholarly achievements in your first year at Evergreen. So I shall conclude this letter by seconding your own concluding sentiments in the voice of the geoduck: "Yes, stop cheating us, and yourself; SPEAK UP."

Ha, ha

Richard

("There lies nothing but grief in love and respect for one's father" — from your paper on Euripides V and Paul's dream. For Moby Dick's sake, I'm going to get you to tell us more about that.)

And to one of our weaker students, last winter, this:

January 31, 1978

Heather M.
Human Development

Dear Heather,

I have just read your self-evaluation for the fourth time, because the first three readings left me at a loss for words. Your self-evaluation is a remarkable document. It is, at once, an English teacher's nightmare and a quite moving personal statement. It answers a question I've been asking myself all year: Why is Heather in this program? Not only have you given me the answer to that question; you have given me a new measure of reassurance about this modern world in which we live, and Evergreen's place in it. The next time I'm in the Sea-Tac Airport parking, I shall remind myself of the possibilities that the person who is taking my money may "know something about human development in psychohistorical perspective," that she may have "liked" *Oedipus Rex,* that she may have understood "half of *Heart of Darkness*" and that, in any event, she may have done "numerous amounts of reading, anyway."

So, I'm glad you are in this program, doing workshops, lectures, seminars, a psychohistory of your mother and reading books you sometimes understand and sometimes don't understand; instead of sitting in the rows of some prebusiness administration course somewhere.

As for now until June: you say, "I feel that I can better my reading by making myself look upon it as fun and not work." You mean fun *as well as* work, don't you? I agree. You say, "In writing I think if I made myself do more of it I might be able to start making some sense." Well, it isn't that you aren't making some sense, Heather. It's that you're mostly making only *personal* sense. You need to try to make *general* sense. Why not try, at the end of each paper, from now on, to answer this question: Now, what does it have to do with everything and everybody? I'm not sure that will work, but it's worth a try I think. You say, "As far as my speaking goes I think I won't force myself to speak. I think I will get further if I don't pressure myself." I agree, while hoping that at some point the general atmosphere of the program will disabuse you of your "terrible fear of saying the wrong thing at the wrong time." It happens from time to time in the seminar, haven't you noticed? And were'e still friends.

Gratefully,

Richard

It is easy to tell when you've written a thoughtful letter of reflection, from when you've written an unthoughtful one. When you write a thoughtful letter of reflection to a student, you get a thoughtful letter of reflection back from that student. For example, from Karen K., this:

Faculty Evaluation
February 6, 1978

Dear Richard:

I just finished *Something Happened*. How could you do that? Well, at least I will not have difficulty being particular about it. I wish I couldn't be particular. It pisses me off.

Reading my evaluation Thursday night was like waiting for my grade in Washington State History my senior year. The teacher (the prick) held out. He luringly waved the report card at me from the front of the room. "Come and get it Kramer . . . It's all yours." He knew what it meant and he was getting all the disgustingly anal sadistic pleasure he could. When I walked up to get it, he flicked it from his fingers. I watched it sail aimlessly to the floor. I was the one with the pain. He had pleasure. The card felt nothing. I bent down to pick it up (it had landed face down). It was what I expected. He sneered. Was it worth it? Is anything all that important? I never felt the same afterward.

That's how I felt Thursday night. I was being held out on. You were holding back. I knew something was going to happen. It didn't. What was I expecting? I can't really say. Perhaps I wanted to read that my work was more than "just fine".

Friday when I re-read it, I felt totally different. I could see you behind the typewritten lines. You were suggesting things. Telling me where I was in need of improvement. You're perceptive. You know what your students need to hear . . . and what they don't. (I guess I didn't really need to know that you approved of my work; it was more important to know it was in need of improvement).

I would suggest, as you already are aware, that you give me pinpoint areas of imparticularity. I think we both reached somewhat simultaneously the root of my writing disabilities.

Now the road is much easier.

I enjoy the program (not particular enough . . .) It's like going to bed in the evening, knowing you did something . . . accomplished something, feeling good and having a nice dream (a little more particular, but not enough). Um, it's like having an ecstatic topic sentence, seeing it develop into an even more ecstatic paragraph and finally into a (hopefully) ecstatic paper (Ta Da!).

Playing the devil, umm?! Well, that's what you do . . . and your damn good. You take chances with your students, yet it's not as risky as all that.

Thank you for your perceptions of my needs. I also realized that I could handle it (it felt good). I'm not afraid of you anymore either (it feels good).

Very Particularly Yours,

Karen

And, from Matt J., this:

February 5, 1978

Richard Jones
Human Development

Dear Richard:

First off, I would like to comment briefly on your letter of January 31. You seem to be under the impression that I have connections with the twelve tribes of Israel. Not true. You see, my mother is not Jewish, so I have connections with only *six* of the twelve.

Secondly, I resent the phrase "putting it baldly . . . " which appears in paragraph three of your letter. This may not be a phrase well chosen in a letter to a guy who has recently said good-bye to over sixteen inches of hair. Kapish?

Finally, I beg you to change the opening sentence of my self-evaluation before the document sees the light of day. I haven't slept a wink since you pointed that out.

Tsaright?
Tsaright!

I am scared of everyone in our seminar. My fear level seems to fluctuate a lot, but I am always scared of someone. (Usually everyone.) I get the willies when I catch a glimpse of Karen K's folder; it heavies me out when Ellen produced a work such as her contribution to the psychohistory guidelines; I am put to shame by every barrage of Mastrangeloian words; I am curious about John and Steve S. (What are they up to?); Steve A. is a hypno-therapist, which makes me *very* nervous; and Heather, Karen L., and Sandy are too quiet for comfort. I am scared of everyone. Especially you.

You are somehow responsible for all of this fear. I'm not sure exactly how, but I think you are. You're pushy. I push myself, but it's on your behalf. For example, you write an evaluation in which you refer to me as "our ace student." Very flattering, but you then go on to write five additional paragraphs which dwell on my weaknesses. Pushy. So I fear. I fear that if I don't improve, I'll get a less-than-great evaluation at the end of the year. It scares the hell out of me.

I think it all started in our conference in the fourth week of school. You said, right off the bat, "Well, this is a trouble-shooting session, and I don't see that you have any troubles that need shot." Not a very pushy line, at first glance. Think about it, though. Even as early as the fourth week of school you left me no direction to go, but down.

Pushy.

From that point on I pushed myself. I had to. I had to fight just to keep the status quo. Things progressed ok for a while; then, all of a sudden, you began to push. Outwardly. You got more and more critical of my writing, and I began to sweat. I thought I was falling.

I didn't want to fall.

I could have developed an ulcer, or something.

So I worked harder.

And then, the clincher. The evaluation, in which you bluntly, yet subtly put me in my place. You picked me apart, bit by bit, on all levels. You threatened to embarrass me in our seminar by pointing an accusing finger at me, in regard to a disconnected seminar. You threatened that the wind will go out of my writing if I don't learn to speak up more. Low blow, Richard. I've got the willies.

And what purpose does this demoralization serve? What can come of this slow, painful torture? What good does it do me to walk the plank of academia, while you laugh ("ha, ha") and poke the sword a little harder into my back?

I'll tell you. It keeps me going and growing. I need it. That subtle little foil of yours will make sure that I make it to grad school. It'll push me right into grad, and I'll appreciate it. (I already do.) That sword is what makes you a great teacher. (A little less lovable, maybe, but a great teacher.)

You must really care. If you didn't care, all six paragraphs of my evaluation would have looked like the first. ("ace," etc.) And then I'd get cocky, uppity, and impossible to live with. I'd stop growing. I'd feel good, but I'd stop growing. And I *wouldn't* have the willies; this would be the tragedy.

You seem to be right in tune with your students' (students's, a la Strunk) needs, and act accordingly. (You must. If you treated Sandy like this she'd have a heart attack. Or worse!) (Maybe you *do* treat us all like this. If this is the case, I can guess why Teresa chose God.)

(His sword is gentler.)

The point is that you know that I intend psychology as a career (somehow), and you help tremendously on the road to that career. When concerned with, rather than style, content in my writing my papers, you comment on content; when I embarass both of us with a sentence such as that which precedes this one, you don't let me live it down; when my writing voice gets fuzzy, you tell me, in no uncertain terms, what needs to be done ("be *our* guest" indeed!); and finally, when a habit of mine stands to hurt me, as well as the rest of the seminar, you make its continuation impossible.

You've helped me immeasurably thus far; you care, and that matters to me.

Fearfully Yours,

Matthew, son of Jacob

The candor that the teacher earns from the students by the example he sets in his letters of reflection doesn't always result in such goodwilled acknowledgements. If I had been unusually perceptive in my work with Karen and Matt, I had for two quarters been unusually dense in my perceptions of Mary Jo. Fortunately, for the both of us, she felt free to bring this to my attention, as follows:

Richard:

I don't feel respect for you. Perhaps my state of feeling let down by you will color my other perceptions. I feel you're almost never honest, and almost always very selfish.

I never once had a conference with you. I never felt quite violently enough distressed or close enough to suicide to ask you for an hour of your time. Yet, I felt so alone and afraid and stuck sometimes. It would have been very helpful to me had you invited, or at least given off an air of openness to casual conversation about the subject matter. Willingness to respond to a student's attempt to make the subject matter a part of their *lived* life, to make it real — not just reserved for official meetings, even official meetings as relaxed as dream reflection seminars.

I've truly felt that it would be an *imposition* to ask you to spend an occasional hour talking to me about an exciting and enigmatic dream I've had, about a piece of Chaucer, or any other reading I've done, about my relations with you, or a personal problem which is getting in the way of my reading, writing, seminaring, or thinking. I feel it's horrible for a student to feel such reluctance towards imposition on the *life* of their teacher! I think some of my feelings of distance from the program have resulted from this.

Why didn't I come and confront you with this? I mentioned it sort of at a potluck and in some writing. I wasn't frank enough — but I wasn't so clear as to how I felt and why. And I just felt too huge a burden to have something IMPORTANT (crucial) with which to pay for your borrowed time. Anyway, you've encouraged and allowed a pretty open and independent seminar. As you know, your difficulty in getting into Chaucer shortchanged us a bit.

Also, as you probably know, your double message about "write what you want and need to for yourself" for the book along with "write what I tell you should" created a lot of problems. Again, my lack of trust.

Perhaps if I had more faith in the signals of my needs and had claimed some right to your support and guidance I would have benefited more highly from you. Perhaps if I were thirty and had met you at a dinner party I would have felt free to appreciate your being an intelligent and nice man.

Sincerely,

Mary Jo

P.S. I gave this letter to my roommate to read after I finished it and she said, "hey now, Mary Jo, some of this sounds too spiteful and sarcastic." I told her that I hadn't meant to be a smartass, but to really try to be honest and clarify my feelings. But then she pointed to my words about IMPORTANT and "pay for borrowed time" and said "*This* is sarcasm. Sarcasm almost never says what it means. Aren't you really saying that you hate him for not giving you enough attention?" I thought about it and concluded that if I hate you, it's as a teacher, and for feeling cheated (not getting enough of the attention I felt I deserved). I hope that this comes through in the letter, untainted. I hope that what may seem like sarcasm does not conceal or detract from the attempted honesty in conveying my feelings.

The two-hour conference, which followed soon after, was mutually clarifying.

TRANSCRIPT EVALUATIONS

Writing formal evaluations for the registrar's records poses a vexing problem if you want to not only meet your responsibilities but also enjoy the writing. To whom are you writing? The student? His parents? Future employers? His next teacher? You can't write to all of these in any voice that you could call your own. I have decided to solve this problem, from now on, by writing the transcript evaluations to the students' next program coordinator, inviting the others to look over our shoulders, as it were. For example, for Karen K., this:

Since this is only the end of Karen's second year of college, rather than address this evaluation to some unknown transcript reader, I shall address it to Professor Priscilla Bowerman, who will coordinate Karen's next program: Introduction to Political Economy.

Priscilla,

Start by reading Karen's final self-evaluation. Have you ever read as moving a statement of achievement in all your years at Evergreen? I haven't. In order to fully appreciate the extent of the drama involved in this particular Evergreen success story, next read my in-house letter of reflection to her of January 26, 1978, in which I rather brutally challenged her to find ways of working in response to her own motives, rather than in response to her perceptions of the teacher's expectations. Next, read the vapid self-evaluation in response to which I wrote the letter, and then read her two spunky responses to my letter — one to herself and one to me. Pretty risky dealings between a student and a teacher, would you agree?

Here is our most prolific and best disciplined student. Where did I get off telling her in her second year of college that she had damned well better learn how to be creative as well? Had it not worked, had Karen not been capable of doing creative as well as dutiful college work, I'd be sitting here writing this evaluation with egg all over my face. But it *did* work, because she *is* capable of creative as well as dutiful college work, and so I get to remember that interchange as one of my more successful teaching feats. How she made it work is told in her own distinctive writing voice in her self-evaluation. And examples of the proof of all of this abound in her prodigious portfolio. (Have you ever seen anything like *that* before? Neither have I.) See especially her interdisciplinary paper on Faulkner's *The Sound and the Fury,* her three (that's right; only one was assigned) psychohistories — one of each of her parents and one of herself — and pp. 48-54 of her "Appendix."

In short, Priscilla, safely expect Karen to be one of your star students next year; as a thinker, yes; as a responsible student, no question; as a writer, most of the time; as a seminar participant, yes, but don't count on her to be much of a talker. And I'd advise you not to push her in this latter matter. She'll develop her speaking skills when and if she wants to. (See her heavily asterisked variations on the theme of concreteness, dated May 22, 1978, for a clue as to why I advise this.)

Karen wants to be a lawyer, and if she doesn't become an exceedingly successful one I shall not believe it. Her choice of your program next year is, therefore, obviously a wise one, You'll enjoy working with her.

In addition to all of the above, she seems to keep a busy extra-curricular schedule, makes her own clothes (which you will also enjoy) and works to pay all of her expenses. She has recently started a wholesale pie-baking company, which shows early signs of being successful.

Now, you may have concluded that Karen will offer no challenges to you as a teacher. Not so. There are two problems of which you should be apprised: (1) For all of the quantity, quality and recent artfulness of her work in college, she does not derive the *personal* satisfaction from it that you or I would derive from it, if we were doing it. In my last conference with her I tried to get to the bottom of this; all I learned was that I'd have to put on my therapist's hat in order to do so — and that isn't in the cards. There is something neurotic as hell in this, but that doesn't make it less real. In fact, it makes it more so for you as her next teacher. (2) For all that the progress she describes in learning to take risks is valid, and for all that she *has* succeeded in giving herself the "second chance" that she speaks of, there will be relapses; and you should be prepared to point them out to her when they occur. She may not always immediately like this, but she will understand what you're doing and why — and she will respond with breathtakingly corrective efforts. For example, that moving final self-evaluation of hers was not her first effort. The first effort was as blah as her mid-year self-evaluation had been. I refused to accept it, told her not to even try to rewrite it, and to compose a new one from scratch. She understood what I meant, and in 28 hours she returned with what you see in her portfolio. As I said, you're going to enjoy working with her.

Suggested course equivalencies (in quarter hours): Total, 48. 4 — Creative Writing; 8 — Expository Writing; 6 — Introduction to Literature; 6 — American Literature; 6 — American Social History; 8 — Psychoanalytic Theory; 6 — Personality Development; 4 — Social Science Research Methods.

What, you may ask, is the Admissions Committee of the Stanford Law School going to think, if and when they should encounter my transcript evaluation of Karen Kramer's second year in college? Well, since it is pointedly addressed to my colleague, Priscilla Bowerman, and not to them, they won't have to think anything of it. They won't, since the document is explicitly not addressed to them, even have to read it, if they don't want to. On the other hand, should they, out of an average expectable amount of voyeuristic motivation, decide it might be fun to read someone else's mail, they will at least go on to read an interesting letter from one recognizable professional to another. And might even go on to decide that a young woman who, as a sophomore, had launched a successful pie-baking business, while also making all of her clothes (which I would never have thought to inform a nonexistent audience) would probably make a good lawyer.

And, for another example, for Matthew J., this:

Since this is only the end of Matt's first year of college, rather than address this evaluation to some unknown future transcript reader, I shall address it to Professor David Marr, with whom he will be studying "American Literature" this summer, and to Professor Leo Daugherty, who will coordinate Matt's program next year, "Shakespeare and the Age of Elizabeth":

David and Leo,

You will immediately recognize Matt's final self-evaluation as one of those rare ones which leave us faculty people in an irritating state of satisfaction. Satisfaction because it is so artfully written, so thorough, and bespeaks such an extraordinary series of achievements — personal as well as academic. Irritating because it leaves the faculty person with so little to say, other than "I confirm it." I confirm it.

Matt and I had a rather awkward year-end conference yesterday for this very reason. With all of my other students, there was plenty for me to advise and to suggest concerning rewriting their self-evaluations. (Why is it that first year students, who have long since demonstrated they are capable of artful and informative writing, tend, when self-evaluation writing time comes around, to relapse into that childish voice with which they usually began?) Matt's was the only exception in my seminars this year. Except for observing that he had used the word "compromise" where he had meant "synthesize," his self-evaluation gave me nothing more to say than "good," "beautiful," "excellent," "type it up on the form."

It was the afternoon before the seventh and final Sonics-Bullets game, and knowing of his interest in sports, I was tempted to raise the subject — but this was supposed to be an *evaluation* conference. So we talked some of his evaluation of the program. (I'm going to Xerox a copy of it for his portfolio. Students tend not to take the writing of program evaluations very seriously, nor as an occasion for festive writing. Matt, charactersitically — now — did. It is the most perceptive one I've seen in years. Don Finkel, who is charged with writing our program history this year, is tempted to submit Matt's program evaluation *as* the program history.)

And then we talked a bit about some of the other students in the seminar who didn't do so well, and why.

Then I asked him if he planned to break the program rule and show his psychohistory of his father to his father (thinking that if I had done as superb a job with such an assignment, I'd be tempted to). He doesn't plan to do this. "Maybe four or five years from now."

Then we chatted on about his anticipations of working with you guys, and how he thought this might help him to prioritize his growing competing interests in psychology, literature and linguistics. (See his dream reflection writing on this subject, which he called "Fast Fish — Loose Fish." It's delightful.)

Then I allowed as how his best short paper had been the one he did on de Beauvoir, in which he makes a very persuasive case that the dutiful daughter in the book is not Simone herself, as is suggested by the title (*Memoirs of . . .*), but ZaZa. He concludes that a literally correct title would be Memor*ies* of a Dutiful Daughter (ZaZa), thus revealing Mem*oirs* of a Dutiful Daughter (Simone), as perhaps the most artful aspect of the book. If no one else has had this idea, I informed him, he might have here a veritably publishable paper. Leo, I told him, would know if anyone else *had* this idea. How so, asked Matt. Is Leo a de Beauvoir expert? No, I replied (knowing you will steal him for your seminar next year, and working up a little advanced transference), Leo just knows *every*thing.

I terminated our abbreviated conference by telling him he'd made as remarkable progress in the first year of college as any student I've known, that if he continues at this rate (which is unavoidable) he'll be doing the equivalent of graduate work in his second year. And that by the time he's a senior he'll be in good position to enroll in the graduate program of his choice in the field or fields of his choice.

Would I set him up for this kind of disappointment if I wasn't positive he'll prove me right?

Suggested course equivalencies (in quarter hours): Total, 48. 4 — Creative Writing; 8 — Expository Writing; 6 — Introduction to Literature; 6 — American Literature; 6 — American Social History; 8 — Psychoanalytic Theory; 6 — Personality Development; 4 — Social Science Research Methods.

But Karen and Matt were two of our best students. Would the same formula work for the run-of-the-mill ones. Why not?

June 14, 1978
Evaluation of Sandra M.

Since this is only the end of Sandra's first year of college, I think it makes better sense to address this evaluation to Professors Peskin, Aldridge and McNeil, with whom she will be working this summer and next year, than to some unknown future transcript reader.

Joye, Bill and Earle:

If my experience with Sandy is any indication, you're going to have to support, support, support. But then you can expect that she will respond with steady improvement. The problem is one of self-confidence. She is a mature woman with two teenage children who decided, with many reservations, to try to acquire a college education. She is an intelligent woman with a good command of the mechanical aspects of the language, who commits her thoughts to speech or written language over enormous inner resistances. She has to learn that her thoughts and opinions can be valuable.

From this point of view she couldn't have chosen a more unfortunate program than Human Development. Not only did the design of the program emphasize scholarly objectives over practical ones, but the majority of the students who enrolled in the program happened to be seasoned students with quite sophisticated educational backgrounds. In the first few weeks she was nearly in a state of shock, feeling that she had made a mistake, that she didn't have what it takes to succeed in college and that she should drop out of school. I had to assure her repeatedly that her performance would not be evaluated on a comparative basis, that she was only expected to move ahead at an acceptable pace from where she herself was. And then I had to almost insist that she give herself this chance. Without these assurances and insistences, which were necessary throughout the year, although in decreasing frequency, she would surely have dropped out.

And that would have been a mistake. Sandy's interests in a college education are practical and career-oriented. What's wrong with that? Nothing, except that Human Development was expressly designed *not* to meet practical, career-oriented needs. The fact that she finished the program and earned full academic credit can only be adequately appreciated in this light.

Writing a psychohistory of her father became a nightmare for her. Not only was it emotionally taxing, but she had simply never before done a major piece of research and writing. And here were other students in her seminar turning in drafts of up to forty pages, when she had yet to complete two! She suffered through several drafts. On one occasion she submitted one of the drafts to a two hour critique by the whole seminar. She finished it. On the last day. It is good. Not inspired. But good. The next such writing effort should come more easily. I urge you to read it. It will reassure you that she merits the support you will have to give her.

She rarely participated actively in the book seminars, but she listened attentively and (more importantly) with genuine pleasure.

The dream reflection seminars were a pleasant surprise to her. She couldn't bring herself to do much of the writing, but she learned the important lesson that a thought doesn't have to be profoundly serious in order to be valuable and interesting.

The change in her relationship with good books is the achievement of Sandy's that is the most pleasant for me to report. She didn't finish all of them (the pace of the program was too fast) but she started all of them, finished many, and is going to finish the rest in her leisure time. Before this year, books by people like Melville, Hawthorne, Kafka, and Faulkner, or by Freud, Kovel, and Slater were, in her view, things that if one read them it was because one *ought to.* Now they are to be read out of desire.

Unfortunately, there is no credit category for that achievement.

Suggested course equivalencies (in quarter hours): Total, 48. 2 — Creative Writing; 2 — Expository Writing; 4 — Introduction to Literature; 4 — American Literature; 4 — American Social History; 4 — Psychoanalytic Theory; 4 — Personality Development; 24 — General Education.

If you don't know what the student plans to do next, there is nothing for it but to turn out one of the kind of tiresome documents that usually get written to nonexistent audiences; but there are usually only a few of these. In the cases of students who are transferring, dropping out or graduating, an advising session (called for in any event) will usually produce some glimmer of an audience. In the cases of students who have chosen a particular graduate program, and for whom you are therefore going to have to write a letter of recommendation anyway, such an advising session affords an opportunity to review the student's complete portfolio and then to compose the kind of personalized recommendation that graduate admissions committees tend to appreciate. For example:

May 5, 1975

Ms. Phyllis Stricks
Director of Admissions
Bank Street College of Education
610 West 112th Street
New York City 10025

Dear Phyllis Stricks,

I am happy to sponsor Terry Bonynge's application for admission to Bank Street. She was in a seminar of mine for half of last year; we have had numerous advisement sessions and have enjoyed a variety of social occasions (potlucks, retreats, etc.) together. So, I know her well.

You may as well know, if you haven't sensed it already, that I take particular pride in the students to whom I suggest Bank Street, and have in fact been very sparing over the years in making the suggestion. Unless I feel sure the student will make outstanding contributions, as for example have Bob Neiderman and Colleen Coleman, I tend to suggest graduate programs closer to home. Terry Bonynge will, I'm sure, add another name to which I can refer when next I write you.

Her special strengths lie in her ability to inspire the confidence of others in her leadership of group activities. In this she is soft-spoken, naturally talented and a hell of a lot of fun. She is also known as a very good friend in one to one relationships, being a good listener as well as outspoken in expressing her own convictions. As a student she does everything well — reading, writing, research and organizing her time. She will take the level of graduate study in stride.

For a time she was intimidated by the small seminar settings she encountered at Evergreen, having come to us from a two thousand student high school and the University of Wyoming where she had never experienced a small class in which students were expected to actually say what they thought. At Evergreen she entered an advanced program in which most of her colleagues were seasoned seminarians. For several months she was the inwardly agonized silent member. However, her confidence in the abilities she manifested outside the seminar setting, reinforced as it was by the appreciation of others, gradually encouraged her to be more assertive in seminars until now she can seminar with the best.

I have seen Terry relate to young children on several occasions and confidently predict that she will be at least as much of an instant success in her internship work as Colleen Coleman probably was.

Although she is by nature very much an outdoors person she has the maturity and resourcefulness to cope creatively with New York City for a couple of years.

Sincerely,

Richard M. Jones, Ph.D
Professor of Psychology

The informality of these transcript evaluations in the form of letters to colleagues is balanced by the necessarily more formal tone of the student's own transcript evaluation. For example:

The Evergreen State College · Olympia, Washington 98505
THE STUDENT'S OWN EVALUATION OF PERSONAL ACHIEVEMENT

Larsen	Lori	Gene	531-74-5273
Student's Last Name	First	Middle	ID Number

Shakespeare and the Age of Elizabeth   1/8/79   6/1/79
Title   Date began   Date ended

Upon entering Evergreen and the Shakespeare program, I was unsure as to what my expectations should be, and to whether they could be attained in a self-motivating environment. I knew from my experience at Reed that I could perform well when pushed, but I was unsure as to whether I could push myself. If these two quarters have taught me anything, it has been that I can finally rest assured that I may safely count on myself to produce from internal, rather than merely external, sources and expectations.

My doubts about Evergreen's academic core were quickly squelched upon my first examination of the course outline and syllabus. The workload kept me busy throughout both quarters, but allowed just enough time for me to explore areas that aroused my interest as the course unfolded. Two such areas which I was fortunate to pursue were the nature of individualism in the 16th century, and 17th century Metaphysical poetry. Each evolved into a major paper, and each served to develop my critical, analytical, and research abilities. I am especially proud of my project on the Metaphysical poets, which I designed myself and pursued on my own. It was rigorous, time-consuming, and very rewarding. I read the original works of the six major poets of the era, and supplemented these with six critical texts on the subject. Doing this was the best possible way to end the year, as studying the age directly following Shakespeare's was, in effect, like shining a light down the pathway he and his contemporaries had walked.

The broadly-based interdisciplinary focus was very new to me. At Reed, I had been trained to think specifically, and to concentrate my efforts in order to do *one* thing *very* well. While this approach can be very beneficial at times, I do not believe that it is the best way to approach undergraduate education. I believe that over-specialization caused me to narrow my field of vision to about one quarter of what I could possibly consider justifiable. I was beginning to have difficulty drawing conclusions and making generalizations. Upon completion of this program, however, I now have more control over this inner "focal" mechanism, and can successfully combine detail with overview. I am sure my writings reflect this (please see portfolio.)

I worked tremendously hard at increasing my reading comprehension this past year, and it has paid off. The variety of reading materials exercised my concentration span, and I found that I was able to wrench more out of the first reading of our last play, *The Tempest,* than I did from all three readings of one of our earlier plays, *Hamlet.* Part of this is due to becoming more at ease with Elizabethan language, metaphor, and symbolism, but for the rest, I take credit.

I was at a bit of a disadvantage entering the program at the beginning of the second quarter, but I overcame this by becoming seriously involved in the Orientation Workshop for students new to the program. In reading the most crucial works from first quarter along with our second quarter assignments, I was able to grasp the main issues of the program theme much more fully, quickly, and efficiently than if I had not taken the time to catch up.

The learning experience itself was exhaustive. Tracing the blossoming of a genius like Shakespeare is an awesome task, but in doing so, one gets a better grasp of the factors that contribute to one being able to blossom at all. The politics of Elizabeth, the innovation of Spenser and Raleigh, the wisdom of Montaigne, the originality and curiosity of Burton, and the scientific forethought of Bacon, together created a climate that allowed and even encouraged genius to thrive. It was not only intriguing to study the growth of self-consciousness and the individual; it was *inspirational* to be glancing into Hamlet's "mirror held up to Nature," and to begin to understand the intricacies that sustained the Elizabethan creative talent.

By far the most valuable aspect of this program was the experience of studying one area from as many different angles as possible; in this case, the literative, the historical, the musical, the artistic, the scientific, and the sociopolitical. One can take two very distinct things away from the college environment; a bank of factual knowledge and personal insights gained from careful thought and study, and/or a model that will allow one to pursue one's academic interests as they arise throughout one's life. This program has offered me a bank of knowledge which will be invaluable in my future studies of literature and the humanities, but it is the *model* for future investigation that I treasure most, and which I have most definitely received from this program. The depth and quality of insight to be gained from the inter-disciplinary model approach cannot be equalled. Neither can the satisfaction of knowing the bounds and limitations once encountered can be overcome by a new perspective . . . an angle I would perhaps have never considered had I not studied this precise subject in this precise manner. I am extremely satisfied with what I have done, and hope that my summer studies of the Romantics will be at least this rewarding.

Lori Larsen	Richard M. Jones
Student's signature	Faculty signature
6/4/79	6/6/79
Date	Date

But even these formal evaluations are sometimes enlivened when a student has had an extraordinarily satisfying year, and has learned to write with confidence:

The Evergreen State College · Olympia, Washington 98505
THE STUDENT'S OWN EVALUATION OF PERSONAL ACHIEVEMENT

Jones	Crystal	Annette	539-48-1363
Student's Last Name	First	Middle	ID Number

Shakespeare and the Age of Elizabeth   10/78   5/79
Title   Date began   Date ended

1964:   "I will not read MacBeth," I said. "I will not waste time decoding unintelligible gibberish."

"That's OK," my English teacher said. "When you're ready, you'll read it."

1979:   Victory!

Shakespeare and the Age of Elizabeth are finally mine. I am no longer intimidated by Bardolatry and iambic pentameter. I know Hamlet better than all my cousins in St. Louis. How did this happen?

Fall quarter it happened by writing. I took a writing mechanics workshop that demanded a paper a week. I produced. Comprehending the home life of commas and semicolons was soothing, predictable, and not up for negotiation. But interpreting Machiavelli as satire, and the *Merchant of Venice* as number symbolism turned into risk and sweat.

Reading was the highlight of my winter quarter. The program question — what makes a culture bloom? an age golden? a Shakespeare great? — whittled itself down to "What makes the Elizabethan language so special?" Owen Barfield's book, *Saving the Appearances,* triggered a profound explosion of ideas. I spent the rest of the year wrestling. What are the connections between form and function, space and time, music and language?

Also in winter quarter, another student and I conducted a six-week seminar to orient new students. The best way to learn is to teach. I knew this intellectually in January. By March, I knew it emotionally. As a teacher, I now view seminars as verbal soccer games and no longer consider silence golden.

The total year's input began to flow out our collective mouths by spring quarter. Our seminar grew into a cohesive band of voices: pushing, dissecting, playing, achieving. It was not only fun to talk, but astounding to experience one person's clarity, another's enthusiasm, or another's special point of view. Fortunately, this energy was contagious. The last material read (Burton, Bacon, Montaigne) lacked continuity and dramatic tension. My emotional investment lagged. I became more interested in my own fresh discoveries (much of it trite, no doubt) than the assigned discoveries of Elizabethan thinkers. I was pulled along by my friends to an anticlimatic end.

The rewrite workshop required even more support and co-operation — a commitment to self and group improvement. To explain how to rewrite a paper was to show how to write. I cannot think of a more effective teaching tool. We outgrew the need for a formal leader, and, in fact, conducted one session without him.

Showing no compulsion to quit talking, I was assigned a lecture on our last play, *The Tempest*. Like Caliban, I found themes reflecting my attempts to grasp what seemed to lay a bit beyond my ability — my vision. Maybe I should have gotten some directional help at this point, but I decided to keep chewing on broad spectrums of material and hope for eventual focus. The lecture was apparently stimulating enough to charge new thought patterns in the audience, but I end the year harboring nomadic bands of restless ideas with no place to go. I can accept this lack of personal closure as strangely successful.

Evergreen worked, in part, because I leave the program with more awareness of what I don't know than what I do know. I am wondering about all the things going on "out there" that I'm missing. I am wondering how to find out about them. I am wondering if it matters if I find out about them. I don't know how to document this kind of success for bureau-crats. But walking out of a state institution carrying minimal frustration, boredom, and a reevaluated self image should be recognized as valuable. Certainly unique.

Crystal A. Jones	Richard M. Jones
Student's signature	Faculty signature
5/31/79	6/7/79
Date	Date

FACULTY SELF-EVALUATION

Don't fall in the trap of trying to write these to yourself — who cannot also be an audience. To do so is to unnecessarily arouse not only your narcissistic impulses, but also your defenses against your narcissistic impulses — a situation not conducive to producing a piece of writing which could interest anyone. Choose someone to whom to address your reflections on the year who could actually be interested in you and your work at Evergreen, and who is not likely to be embarrassed by these annual exhibitionistic indulgences. Some faculty choose to write their self-evaluations to their dean. I have never thought that this might be enjoyable. In the early days I used to write them to the other members of my faculty team. Lately, I've taken to writing them to friends to whom I owe a letter anyway, who also have some interest in Evergreen. The last one I wrote to Lee and Leo Daugherty who were on sabbatical at Oxford. The one before that I wrote to Tom Maddox, who taught with us in Dreams and Poetry, and who was at the time on the East Coast in graduate school. The one before that I wrote to Eugenia Hanfmann, a friend and former mentor of mine.

What one chooses to write about in one's self-evaluation, and how one chooses to center the document, tends to be a function of the number of one's years here. In my first year, I stuck pretty close to the actual teaching skills I was trying to develop: program designing, seminar leadership, lecturing, faculty seminaring, advising, etc. Now I find myself focusing my reflections on some event, or motif or discovery that feels like the year's psychological center of gravity. Each year I have found myself to be a little less interested in my "faculty development" than I was the year before. It is, however, an annual professional commitment, in the importance of which

I strongly believe, so the only way I have continued to find enjoyment in writing them is to see them as occasions for trying to do some stylish writing. In the beginning I had little to be proud of, but I'm getting better. For example, here are some excerpts from my first one, written on December 17, 1971:

I feel very good about the teaching so far. The most effective I've ever done. All the things I have theorized and preached about over the years, but never been sure were actually achievable — about the role of self-knowledge in the educative process, about the need for integrating insights and outsights, about the importance of inviting affective and cognitive experience, and about the creative role of authority in facilitating all this — have proven out. They are realizable in a public school. Most of the credit, of course, goes to the design features of the program — the eleven to one seminar ratio, the absence of competing demands on student time, the tightness of structure regarding content and looseness of structure regarding process, the weekly dose of real responsibility that most of the students get in their internships, the absence of excessive reading and writing assignments, the explicit commitments to self-study and work-study as well as book study, and the weekly opportunities provided for the faculty to enjoy the intellectual stimulation of colleagues. But I can say, for myself, that I think I took good advantage of these conditions.

Moreover, I feel that every bit of my skill and experience was required in the process. For example, I have for years tried to follow the rule, learned from Dr. Semrad, that the function of a group's leader is to do for the group, as a group, at any given moment, what no one else is doing for it at that moment; whether this be talking or listening, observing or participating, analyzing or relating, challenging or supporting. This quarter I followed that rule with consistent success. However, so engaged was I in doing this that I was almost never conscious of trying to follow a rule — which, as I discovered when I was doing psychotherapy, is when you know you've arrived. So much for how I feel.

What are the signs that the seminars are going well?

(1) From the beginning the students have talked primarily to each other. They are never unaware of my presence; indeed, the tension that characterizes the social atmosphere of any group in the presence of authority is palpable from week to week. Yet, awareness of this tension has rarely been mentioned, so intent have the students been in communicating with each other, which they are doing with dramatically increasing skill, responsibility and mutual affection. . . .

(4) The students' expressions of attitudes and feelings toward me show just that constancy on the individual level, and inconstancy on the group level, that I have learned indicates authority is serving and not hindering their development. With each individual student there has developed a more or less constant bond of warmth and mutual respect. In the seminars, however, the same student may regard me in the course of a single meeting with suspicion, trust, comfort, anxiety, dislike, admiration, pride and guilt. No student has consistently regarded me in the seminars as he has outside the seminars. Nowhere is this more dramatically visible than in the terms by which I am variably addressed in the seminars. "Dick," "Richard," "Jones," "you," "he," "Mr. Jones," "Dr. Jones." Authority, I have found, tends to have these identity problems. Authoritarianism, on the one hand, and comradeship on the other, are not so difficult to name. . . .

In sum, I think the evidence is strong that the students are moving nicely toward the Program's objectives. They are learning to interpret their lives to themselves and to each other, in response to representative books in the Social Sciences and Humanities, and in relation to responsible work in the Community.

There is one other sign. I feel that I have done a little growing myself, and I'd like to go into that next. In one of my early journal entries (June 25, 1971, and relaxing at Hvar) I find this statement: "Why has Evergreen come to mean so much to me? Because it may afford an opportunity to develop something in myself, in my work, that just wasn't getting called for at Brandeis, Santa Cruz or Harvard. To teach, as effectively or more so, without the pose, without the deadening distance.

Not without the authority but without the self-deceptions that being an authority has frequently involved elsewhere. Big words then. Because I had no way of knowing then what they would come to mean. Some of it has taken me by surprise. . . .

But why then, if the teaching is going so all-fired well, am I not more happy with the job. Why can Sluss so often ask, with his typical accuracy, "Hey, Dick, are you feeling down about things?" It is vexing on these occasions not to have the hours it would take to explain to him how it is that the answer is yes, about almost everything but the teaching. The goddamn building, budget, college, phone, 24-hour day, times, world, lack of contact with last year's friends and their programs, Angyal's book being out of print . . . very little of which is germane to the task at hand. Even in respect to the task at hand, however, there are doubts which contribute to the general unhappiness, and yet, paradoxically, also contribute, by way of their opposition, to the general feeling of well-being about the teaching:

There are times when I am conscience-stricken by the thought that these students would probably perform poorly on subject matter tests in biology, psychology, anthropology, etc., compared to a group of freshmen at the University who were taking courses in these areas. I have to remind myself that what the freshmen at the University would be demonstrating by their superior test performances would not be lasting learning but temporary memorization, and that what these twenty-two people are learning is being integrated into their personal lives. Then, I think, but all you may be doing is providing a comparaeively nondestructive alternative to what they'd have had at the University — a neutral rather than a minus experience. Then, I think, what is so neutral about personally integrated learning? And so it goes, back and forth. Harvard, it seems, dies slowly.

There are times when the students' complaints get to me that I am too distant, that I don't participate more, that I don't allow myself to become one of them, that they don't know me, etc. I have to remind myself that these complaints, while honestly felt and well intended, are also attempts by them to forfeit the challenge of taking themselves and our objectives seriously, by getting me to do the same. Moreover, I do participate in their seminars, as I think will eventually be appreciated, when they come to trust their own perceptions. . . .

Two and a half years later, needing an audience with whom I could be both more expansive and more specific:

April 3, 1975

Dear Genia,

Angyal has been occupying a lot of my thoughts of late, as he usually does at the end of these Evergreen programs. Once again the students' response to the book was enthusiastic. Almost without exception, they singled it out in their self-evaluations as the most personally valuable psychology book to which they had ever been exposed. But, more than that, there is something about the experience of writing a thoughtful self-evaluation at the end of one of these programs that elicits a vividly living example of the universal ambiguity principle, as the two systems compete for control of the reflective process: Did I really achieve this or that, or was I merely engaged in skillful self-deception? Did I really contribute to the success of the seminar, or was I getting a free ride? Are all these new questions I had about life and about me signs of becoming an educated person, or are they merely more indices of my basic indecisiveness? That sort of thing.

Here's an amusing example that I shall treasure: These past two quarters I have been working full time with twenty students in a program entitled Psychology, Literature and Dream Reflection. It was the most richly satisfying educational venture I've ever been involved in. The students had written their self-evaluations and were reading portions of them to each other in our last seminar meeting. After reading an extremely flattering statement (flattering to herself, to her fellow students and to me) one girl said: "And now I have an embarrassing confession to make. When I was writing my self-evaluation and trying to remember all the things we've achieved I kept remembering what Richard told us was going to happen at our first meeting last September. So, I got out my notes and this is what he said: "You are going to learn the psychoanalytic and holistic theories of human development in ways you'll never be able to forget. You are going to read Shakespeare and other great writers with an entirely new set of eyes. You are going to learn more about yourselves and each other than perhaps you presently care to know. You will come to regard your own writing as a potential source of immense satisfaction. And you will find yourselves working your asses off and loving every minute of it, not because you'll have to but because you'll want to." And then he lays this detailed schedule on us: every book, every lecture, every assignment, every seminar — even the potlucks and retreats — everything planned ahead of time, before he even met us. And now, six months later, everything he said was going to happen has happened. And I'm really glad. I'm even grateful to Richard, cause I could never have thought up that particular combination of things myself. And I have to recognize that all he did was plan the program for us. Beyond that he didn't make it work for us; we made it work for ourselves. But somehow, I can't help feeling a little pissed, too, like I was being manipulated all along without knowing it! It's a really weird kind of mixed reaction." You can easily imagine, Genia, I'm sure, the special delight with which I saw this as an occasion to ask the seminar if anyone could recall anything from Angyal's book that would explain this "weirdly mixed reaction" of Elena's. And you can also, I'm sure, appreciate the artistic satisfaction with which I listened to the ensuing discussion, and watched the last vestige of Elena's transference dissolve into the real working relationship that had been growing between us but only stabilized its dominance at this very last minute. (The more satisfying, I should add, in that I did not articulate the experience in these technical terms until I sat down just now to share it with you. I'm truly grateful for all that you and Angyal taught me about psychotherapy. But I am now positive, having had the opportunity these past four years to practice what I used to only preach, that the natural setting for the psychotherapeutic art is the classroom, where personal insight can be acknowledged as *a means* toward the end of achieving a deeper and more lasting education. As you know, I've been saying something like that in books and articles now for about fifteen years, but only in this past year have I experienced what I meant in such ways as to dispel all doubt as to its truth. Truth? Did I say "truth?" The pause needs explaining. Another of the things I enjoy about teaching at Evergreen is that I get to do a lot of reading outside of psychology. For example, my readings this past year in Polanyi, Wittgenstein and Marshack have convinced me that one of the dumbest illusions Historical Man has conned himself into is that there is such a thing as truth. When, in reality — human reality, that is — all there ever have been and ever will be are more and less interesting stories that we make up, in order to orient and entertain ourselves through life. So, change that to now I am sure that psychotherapy as an aspect of teaching makes for the telling of more interesting stories than does psychotherapy for its own sake.) . . . .

(We spent an evening with Andrew and Dara — and that crazy dog — recently, and Andrew showed me some snapshots of you celebrating your seventieth birthday. I'd like to think that if and when I reach seventy, I shall be as alert and full of life as you obviously are. Which reminds me: how old was I when we first met at Harvard? It was my first year there, when I was twenty-five. That means you were only forty-five; younger than I am now, and you seemed so venerable then! I'm happy to notice that that bit of transference, too, has since dissolved into a friendship which is at least as valuable to me now as was the awesome teacher I needed you to be then.)

I find that keeping an evolutionary perspective is becoming increasingly important to me. I've been interested in what little is known about human evolution as far back as I can remember, but it's always been a largely academic interest, something I called on when preparing a lecture or when leading a seminar or just having an intellectual conversation. Recently I have noticed it becoming important to me *personally,* in the ways I experience day to day living, to acknowledge that the period of history into which I was born and in which I continue to live is one of many; that Norman O. Brown is probably right in his claim that history itself, founded as it is on repression of death, is one prolonged social neurosis, and that the neurosis may be approaching a state of bankruptcy in the very times in which I live. And so on. Polanyi speaks to this view; Marshack's illuminating new archeological findings support it; Freud, of course, foreshadowed it — as did Shakespeare and Chaucer in their times, and it is echoed in our own time I think by Joseph Heller in *Catch-22* and *Something Happened*. This is not the place to detail the perspective itself. I only want to note that it has become of personal importance to me to live in this perspective, i.e., to assume some personal responsibility viz-á-viz the society and times into which I happened to be born. And as I seek to assume this responsibility — not, of course, in the sense of thinking I can undo or change anything on a societal scale, but only in the sense of evaluating what I think, what I feel and what I do in respect to the best historical judgements I can make — those two systems Angyal speaks of are right in there, trying to call all the perceptual shots. There have been days, for example, when I have felt alternatively depressed and guilty and then cheated and angry: "What's the use! It's futile. Best get it over with." "But why me? Why couldn't I have been born 10,000 years ago? Shit!" You know. But there are other days (most of them, I'm happy to report) when with Herman Melville I see it all as one incredibly good joke, and one that is getting funnier all the time. Could anything be more interesting than trying to live a humane life in utterly inhumane conditions? But Gully Jimson says it better to the Nun in the last lines of *The Horse's Mouth:*

> "Please don't talk," said the nun. "That's all right, mother," I said, "they can't hear me because of the noise of the traffic and because they aren't listening. And it wouldn't make any difference if they did. They're too young to learn, and if they weren't they wouldn't want to." "It's dangerous for you to talk, you're very seriously ill." "Not so seriously as you're well. How don't you enjoy life, mother. I should laugh all round my neck at this minute if my shirt wasn't a bit on the tight side." "It would be better for you to pray." "Same thing, mother."

One example will have to suffice: Everytime I see what powerful effects Angyal's book has on people I have to battle back a whole slew of neurotic inclinations: "God damn John Wiley & Sons!" "What rotten luck that Ierardi died when he did!"

"But you and I didn't help with that dumb title!" "To think of the millions of people who are reading Rogers and Perls — inferior books by comparison — and almost nobody has even heard of Angyal!" Etc. But within the perspective I've been speaking of, the lack of notoriety surrounding Angyal's work becomes something I can actually prize. He had a damned good story to tell; we told it for him rather well; and it has been heard and appreciated. Enough. What would Angyal have had to do to become a popular theorist? He'd have had to start a "school," gone on TV, allowed himself to be worshipped, been a guru — and you and I would have had to become known as "Angyalian analysts." Ugh! Sounds like rationalization, and maybe it is. What I know is that the first reaction gets me down and the second makes me laugh. And with Gulley, I'd rather go out laughing than saying prayers. . . .

With love,

Dick

COLLEAGUE EVALUATIONS

These I find to be the most enjoyable of all, albeit the most time time consuming. With rare exceptions you are writing to a person who has by now become a respected colleague. The two of you have had the extraordinary (for college teachers) opportunity of becoming intimately familiar with each other's styles. For a significant part of a whole academic year, usually, the vitality of the same professional venture has centered your respective work lives. You've had your differences and have probably resolved most of them. You've learned some things from the other and seen the other learn some things from you. It's probably not in the cards that the two of you will soon again find yourselves on the same team. Under the circumstances, it is as likely you could stand on ceremony, or indulge false pretenses, as you could kiss your wife's (or husband's) hand. It is a time, in other words, for an exchange of professional intimacies.

Here is what I wrote last year to a colleague with whom I had previously been in public opposition in a painful faculty termination appeals case:

February 21, 1978

Colleague Evaluation
David Marr
Human Development, 1977–78

Dear David,

1

I had to look up "antinomian," in order to know how to respond to your dumping on my dream poet there; and now, like it or not, I have to admit his nationality. Yes, I guess he is an American, because he's all faith. If you believe in him, he's sound; if you don't, he's unsound. Sure there's an unbridgeable gap between unconscious processes and conscious ones. The trick is in bridging that gap (integrating the primary and secondary processes, as we say in the shop). Making believe there's a dream poet turns that trick. So I choose to be antinomian about him, and let his soundness be damned. Anyhow, what matters is that "the crabbed, lobotomized style of their official academic writing gives way to a fluent idiomatic style . . . " You do agree with that much, I know; and it has been one of the special delights of this year for me to have seen that you do. (It was very important to me that David Marr not turn his hard nose up at my dream reflection seminar.)

2

" . . . meaningless but accurate." I agree, but I want to dwell on your choice of words there, because I think another man would probably have chosen other words. I think, Dave, that your distinctive brand of intellectual life, your essential identity as a teacher, is somehow poised by the tension between meaning and accuracy (as mine, I think, is similarly poised by the tension between interest and truth — and it occurs to me that those two sets of terms may be mighty close to being synonomous). It is amazing how alike you and I are in the values which govern our teaching, and which define our relationships to Evergreen. Yet, I think we come to those almost identical positions by way of quite different organizations of that tension between interest/meaning and truth/accuracy. I go around saying "I don't care if it is true as long as it's interesting," knowing that untruths are almost never interesting, and so I go to great lengths to be sure that the students at least mean what they say. You, coming from the other end, go around insisting on accuracy, accuracy, accuracy; yet you'll accept inaccuracies all over the place if you feel they are leading the student toward something meaningful. For example, Jessica decoded the essence of your teaching style when she said, "Intentions are not enough for you." But then she went on to say, "You calmly accepted my shortcomings and goings and quietly mentioned tools I could use to clarify my thoughts. . . . It involves courage to accept the bad with the good and knowing things often turn out differently than what you expect." She's got your number, that Jessica. Love at first sight, indeed.

3

You're an elitist working at a school in which half the students are barely literate, and you are loving it. Ha ha ha ha. I thought of suggesting that some year you arrange an exchange with someone in the English department at Brandeis, where a student can't enroll unless he's not only literate but highly so. So as to have at least one year in which to indulge your elitism. But, no, I thought, if Dave wasn't surrounded by reading and writing problems, he'd be bored silly.

4

Jeff Lovelace is full of shit. You do *not* need to be more dynamic and less low key. Your dynamism, and it is palpable, is centered precisely in your low keyedness. Jeff may be right that some students need to be tricked into learning, but what he doesn't seem to have realized is that behind that characteristic eyes-only smile of yours is one of the best tricks going on here at Evergreen. As you say, "Some lectures have to fail in order to succeed."

5

"Language never takes care of itself."

You can say that again, brother, as you surely will hundreds of times, but you won't have to say it to me again, because I have got the message, and I got it from you here this year and I shall not forget it.

This has involved one of the biggest (both sad and funny) double takes of my Evergreen career. I have known and believed and said out loud repeatedly, for years, that good writing is the heartbeat of the modern educational process. Oh, how I have said this! When the good wriitng was there, I would say, "Hey gang, look at this good writing, let's have some more." And when it wasn't there, I would say, "Hey, gang, come on, let's have some good writing. Please? Some good writing? Try. Come on. Please?" Naturally (naturally, my ass), I meant that they should do the good writing at home and bring it to school. It just never occurred to me, until this year, that college students should be allowed to try to write good right there in the mother fucking classroom — where I, the teacher, could help them! Jesus, I'm 52 years old and have been in the racket half my life and I have known, for sure, that until a student starts to write well not much else of educative consequence can happen to him in school — and it still didn't crack my dimwitted Harvardian consciousness that it might be wise to devote some classroom time to writing! And the dawn didn't come easily, either. I remember, when you started your Wednesday writing workshops, thinking to myself: How nice. And when you sprung them on the whole program — on company time — I didn't know what to think. Can we afford this? Won't the students complain? Should we be treating them like children like this? But they didn't complain; they were grateful. Sure we were treating them like children. *Starved* children. And they ate it up. Of course! And I won't forget it. I won't be able to lecture about writing as you do. And I'll never learn the vocabulary of writing-teaching. But I don't think I'll need to. All I needed to learn was *it is worth the time. Classroom* time. The rest I can play by ear. Thanks.

6

Some zap lines from your letters:

"I wonder if you know how American you are."

"I know this: I'd be no good to you as a friend."

"Going through the motions can be treacherous, and much more work than real learning is."

"I'm not at all surprised that it's struck you like a revelation — that paying attention to predication is the golden key to learning.

7

I deeply appreciated your letter to Evans supporting my attack on the windmills last quarter. As I said in my letter to Lee and Leo, I think I got me a few.

8

Negatives? Only one, and it has to do not with you in this program but with you at TESC over the years: at times I think you have been unreasonably intolerant of our brothers and sisters down at the other end of the log — the experiencers of experience. Now, as I trust you have sensed, I happen to agree with your aristocratic tastes in these matters. I, like you, if I could change the world, would not leave room in it for that style of teaching. But they exist, and, you know, it *is* a free country after all. Those people *are* serving a clientele, which *is* a part of the citizenry of this democratic state for which we work, which is what forces me to see this as a question of taste rather than one of philosophy. As long as they don't complain about your *not* running group process seminars, where do you get off complaining that they *do* run them? There are some not so covert considerations behind this criticism: 1) I used to do some of that kind of teaching myself, and look at me now. So, there's hope, right? 2) If it weren't for the group processers, their students might be looking for me. So take it easier on my bodyguard, will you?

9

Dave, my overall estimation of you as a colleague can be summed up by saying that now, in retrospect, I am ashamed I ever raised the question of whether we should try to work together after "the case" last summer. I didn't know it then, and was just trying to play things safe, but I know now that with as dedicated a professional as you are such a question need never have been asked.

Sincerely,
Richard

And David's to me:

February 21, 1978

Evaluation of Richard Jones
by David Marr

Dear Richard,

Hemingway was surely right when he said that the difference between the rich and the poor is that the rich have more money. He was right because when *Hemingway* distinguished the rich from the poor (in this bare way) you got an image of two entire ways of life being contrasted — not just two piles of money, one big and the other small.

It's the rich man in you, I suspect, that is speaking in your self-evaluation. The child of the family before the 1929 crash? Or, at the other end of your personal history, is it the would-be analyst with his small, lucrative, private practice on Cape Cod? (I'll never forget those words: "small, lucrative, private practice.") No wonder you're a cosmic pessimist: you can afford to be. It is the poor who are drawn to cosmic optimism: they almost have to be.

I think you and I proved something to each other this year — after last summer, it was asking too much of either of us that we should go ahead and work together, as originally planned. Yet neither of us was about to sign off from the *Human Development* program. I suspect your motive for continuing was the same as mine: the program (indeed, programs) was more important than individual differences of the sort that surfaced in the appeals case. We are by temperament and philosophy very different, but we do agree on one thing: coordinated studies is what makes Evergreen unique and good. We may never be friends, but we have shown we can work together — and do it amicably, to use one of your favorite words — and that's enough for me.

Why don't you talk in your self-evaluation about your *performance* in the *Human Development* program? Don't give me a Marcusean rejoinder; I know his concept of the performance principle as well as you do (probably better). Is it the rich man's disdain again? Or false modesty? Your performance merits being desublimated forthwith; it's presently entombed in your prose style, or should I say, your prose *manner* ("Shall we give it a title? Let's. We'll call it: *Views from the Nucleus of a Mutant Cultural Gene.*") Freudian baroque?

I'm not squeamish. Your performance has been indispensable to the success of this program. (No, I'll not avoid a good old capitalist word like "success": the socialist revolution doesn't begin in Evergreen coordinated studies, no matter how "co-operative" they may be.) The first day, as we all looked over our seventy-five students mysteriously shrunken over the weekend to fifty-five, you gave a masterful introduction to the *Human Development* program: a beautifully clear outline of the aims and structure of the program, explained in an authoritative but not forbidding tone of voice. It was the best introduction to a program I've heard.

I've learned from your lectures, but what I've learned differs significantly, I'm certain, from what most of the students have learned. No doubt this is always the case. But like all of us, perhaps most especially like me, you have missed the audience as often as you've hit it in your lectures. You've presupposed a degree of intellectual sophistication and a background knowledge of psychology and other subjects which most of our students don't have — even now, let alone back in October when you lectured on dreams and the dream poet. I think this presupposition is in the interests of students, faculty, and coordinated studies.

Three reasons. First, it is impossible to get around the problem of the diffuse audience at Evergreen; it will always consist of a Mastrangelo and a Jacobson (if our luck holds) outnumbered twenty-to-one by the S. S's, S. M's (for whom thanks too, but for different reasons), and (gasp) S. H's, C. S's, and J. H's. Second, it is better to go over their heads than between their legs (at least the former is not a screwing). Third, it is vital that as colleagues we hear each other speak — and not just in faculty seminar — about matters of intellectual substance.

I'm saying all this, not because I think you may not know it or not agree with it, but, on the contrary, because I know you know it. It's so much a part of your day to day work that you don't see it — or at least don't feel inclined to articulate it. But it comes out, for instance, in your questions and comments following lectures and in other all-program discussions (including faculty seminars in the round). You say things like, "Dave, you've just explained something to me about Riesman and Kovel that I didn't understand before," or, during a lecture of your own, "Don, I know you're not going to accept what I'm going to say, but. . . . " Such comments help weld a program together. They create an atmosphere of commonality within which students have a better than even chance of dealing effectively with ideas introduced by the faculty. Put all this together in a coordinated studies program — the inevitability of missing the audience, but in an atmosphere that makes common inquiry possible — and you get Ellen Brucker saying what she said about your lecture on Angyal. We miss the *audience* and hit the *person* — and that's what education is all about, as far as I'm concerned.

Faculty seminar with you has been a pleasure — and a steady source of stimulation. It's instructive to work with a social scientist who's able to follow his interest without reducing literature to social science. I've learned about Freud by talking with you about Conrad, Shakespeare, and Hawthorne. (I am amused, however, by your stubborn insistence upon finding some "healthy" feature in Kafka; there is none; precisely therein, say I, lies his meaning.)

I like the way you act as coordinator; you take command (everyone seems pleased with how well) by coming with agenda, and you aren't petty (sometimes backhanded compliments are quite appropriate).

We all failed on one significant point of program business, however: we should never have deferred to the indefinite future making a decision about seminar switching; that should have been clearly spelled out in the covenant from the beginning.

Two features of the program design, developed on the run fall quarter, I attribute to your good sense and imagination: the idea of the Psychohistory Guidelines and the plan calling for students to complete the first drafts of their psychohistories by mid-year rather than later. I think these were master strokes.

I can't tell much from your letters of reflections to your students, or from their evaluations of you, how your seminar went fall quarter. And I steadfastly refuse to rely on hearsay. Nor does your self-evaluation discuss your seminar.

But considered as academic advising letters, your LORS are always intelligent and clever, sometimes brilliant (the one to Steve A. is marvelously paced), and almost always these letters (and presumably the conference following) evoked (or provoked) a reply in the student that indicated he had learned something significant. Matt's letter is the finest piece of writing I've seen by a freshman student ever. I wonder if there's such a thing as a Freudian gene.

Most impressive to me, though, was your incisive analysis in the LORS of each student's writing. I know you'll probably maintain until the last day that there are huge differences between our respective approaches to teaching writing, but for my part I know that we're very close, my emphasis on the grammatical basis of rhetoric to the contrary notwithstanding. It's not that there's any virtue in our having a common approach to teaching writing; it's just that I think we've made too much of the differences. You talk about writing the same way I do, for the most part. The main thing is that we both get through to students and actually help them improve. But I loathe the term "zap line." Disneyland.

One final thing: thanks for suggesting that I bring in my *Catch-22* essay to the faculty seminar; I intend to do that just as soon as Word Processing and I get straightened around.

Lieben und arbeiten,

David Marr

PROGRAM HISTORIES

Although the writing of the program history is the joint responsibility of the faculty team, the best ones seem to be those for which one member of the team takes primary responsibility. Here's an example:

PROGRAM HISTORY

for

DREAMS AND POETRY:
Advanced Interdisciplinary Studies
in Psychology and Literature

Leo Daugherty

1973–74

1) Introduction.

Writing this Program History for Dreams and Poetry is probably
unnecessary. Most of the important things are said in our
Program Description and there is little likelihood that the
program will be repeated again by different faculty, thus
eliminating the traditional Evergreen option of writing for
future planners. Yet it is true that certain successes and failures
are probably worth mentioning, just for the record. The most
important things here, to my way of thinking, were our successful program innovations, and it is to these that I will pay the
most attention. First, the program Description:

Title of Coordinated Studies Program: Dreams and Poetry:
Advanced Interdisciplinary Studies in Psychology and Literature.

Level of Scholarly Work: Advanced.

Credit: 4 Evergreen Units (16 quarter hours) for each quarter
completed in the Program. Total credit for the academic year's
work will be 12 Evergreen Units (48 quarter hours), with the
Program's duration being three quarters.

General Content Description for the Academic Year 1973–74:
This academic Program has focused on the problem of relating
the disciplines of psychology and literary study through concentration on an issue-generating phenomenon indigenous to
both: the interrelating vicissitudes of imaginative expression
and repression. The publication of student written works cen-
tering on this problem is the ultimate aim of our Program;
thus, it is a task-oriented learning situation, with each student

being engaged in a research project representing an aspect of the investigation.

The Fall Quarter (Fall, 1973): The quarter focused, in terms of content, upon the poetry of Geoffrey Chaucer and the writings of Sigmund Freud. Chaucer was chosen because: 1) his work is in many ways ideal for a study of the dream and the writing it generates; 2) his work provides us with the opportunity to relate our studies to a remote time and place — a fascinating exercise in its own right, but also one which provides students with the opportunity to investigate a major writer and his *milieu*. Freud's body of work was chosen because of its obvious seminal importance to psychological investigation in general and to an exploration of dreaming in particular. Books read during the quarter included: *Chaucer's Poetry,* ed. E. T. Donaldson (text in Middle English); Hussey, Spearing and Winny, *An Introduciton to Chaucer;* E. T. Donaldson, *Speaking of Chaucer;* B. H. Bronson, *In Search of Chaucer;* C. S. Lewis, *The Allegory of Love;* Marc Bloch, *Feudal Society;* Michael Polanyi, *Personal Knowledge;* Brewster Ghiselin, ed., *The Creative Process;* Richard M. Jones, *The New Psychology of Dreaming;* Sigmund Freud, *The Interpretation of Dreams.* For balance and to keep in touch with contemporary literature, we read Henry Miller's *The Tropic of Capricorn* and Joseph Heller's *Catch-22.* The heaviest concentration of reading was upon Chaucer's dream-vision poems, his *Troilus and Criseyde,* and selections from *The Canterbury Tales.* The quarter featured weekly lectures by members of the college from outside the Program. These lectures were successful in their attempt to bring the concerns of the various disciplines to bear on the problems under investigation. The lectures dealt with such related areas as modern philosophy, political science, and medieval literature. The quarter also featured two all-day seminars per week, one in literature and one in dream reflection and creative writing. The latter is a new educational method with which several members of the program faculty have been experimenting in recent years. In essence it seeks to conjoin the principles and disciplines of dream interpretation with those of aesthetics and literary criticism, with the aim of facilitating cross-fertilization of the students' growing mastery of personal and public knowledge. In addition, public *faculty seminars* were held weekly on the books and topics generated by the inquiry, and many individual conferences were held each day between faculty members and students.

The Second Quarter (Winter, 1974): The quarter focused on project-centered research. Each of the students in the program, having chosen an individual project of an advanced nature within the areas of psychology and/or literary studies, embarked on a course of bibliography — compilation, research, and writing. Instruction was carried on through individual conferences, project-centered seminars, continuing seminars in dream reflection, and lectures. The ongoing component of public faculty seminars continued to function on a weekly basis as described above.

The Third Quarter (Spring, 1974): During Spring Quarter, the program continued working toward its preestablished goals. Individual research projects were completed one by one, and the book publication project moved into the final editing stage under the direction of Dr. Sinclair. Negotiations for publication are underway. Program components continuing from previous quarters included the two-day dream reflection seminars and the weekly "open" faculty seminar. To these were added a weekly poetry seminar and a weekly lecture series on poetry and aesthetics. Poets studied included Shakespeare, Coleridge, Keats, Blake, Wordsworth, and Theodore Roethke. Visiting lecturers included the poet Diane Wakoski, the critic Morse Peckham, and Evergreen faculty members from outside the program. The quarter ended with a one-week evaluation retreat at the Fort Worden Conference Center in Port Townsend, Washington, followed by a three-day, all inclusive, final examination.

Faculty: Richard M. Jones, Ph.D. (Psychology); Thomas Maddox (Teaching Associate, Literature); Leon R. Sinclair, Jr., Ph.D. (English); Leo Daugherty, Ph.D. (Literature and Linguistics), Coordinator.

2) History of the Innovations.

We were forced into being innovative above and beyond NEEAC (Normal Evergreen Experimentation and Creativity) because our original plan for the program fell through. We had applied for a NEH grant for this program, one of the central purposes of which was to reduce the student-teacher ratio to ten to one. When we were left with the normal ratio, we went to work on finding ways to deal with it, while still refusing to give up on our original concepts and goals. Some of the things we came up with follow.

3) The Teaching Associate.

We asked for an extra thousand dollars, at the beginning of the academic year, to pay for the services of an Evergreen student we had known for a long time, Tom Maddox. It would take a long time here to go into Tom's special qualifications; besides, most people here know about them, and they are on record in several other places. Deans Teske and Youtz okayed this request, and Tom went to work for us, functioning as a regular faculty member in the program. (He was paid a total of one thousand dollars, plus some help with tuition and books, for three-quarter's work. He also received full credit as a student in the program.) With Tom, we were able to lower the ratio to fifteen to one, and Tom performed spectacularly for us all year.

4) Visiting Evergreen Lectures.

Each week during the fall quarter, and occasionally thereafter, our program received lectures by various members of the Evergreen literature faculty on Chaucer, the Middle Ages, and theories of poetry. We are extremely grateful to these people for taking the time to help us out, especially since the lectures were so uniformly excellent. I'd like to list them here, just for the record: David Powell, Nancy Allen, Charles Teske, Charles McCann, Beryl Crowe, Richard Alexander, Thad Curtz, Peter Elbow, and Will Humphreys.

5) Outside Lecturers.

We invested quite a bit of our budget in outside people. Among them were Ken Kesey, the Co-Respondents, Morse Peckham, and Diane Wakoski. These expeditures were well worth it, since our students responded not only interestedly, but excitedly, in all cases. With the exception of Kesey (who got a completely favorable response here), these outside speakers also stirred up controversy in our program, thus providing some important issues to focus on.

6) All-Day Seminars.

We had an all-day seminar on Chaucer and an all-day seminar on dream reflection each week. We would break for lunch and then return for the rest of the afternoon. The mornings were given over to discussions, while the afternoons were used to read our writing aloud to each other. (The lunch breaks included an extra hour for purposes of writing responses to the morning discussions.) This worked very well, but grew wearying after ten or eleven weeks, so we went to one all-day seminar for a while.

7) All-Day Faculty Seminars.

We spent one whole day per week on our faculty seminars. The morning was used for reading, writing, and preparation, since our seminars usually focused on a position paper brought in by a faculty member. The afternoon was used for the seminar itself. Our faculty seminars were the best I've experienced so far.

8) Our Weekly Schedule.

Monday was our "Preparation Day," normally called a "Down Day" at Evergreen. This worked out really well for me, since, as coordinator, it gave me a real jump on the week. I could come in on Monday and clean up most of the busywork and other paper junk at my leisure. My suggestion to all future program coordinators is to make Monday the Down Day. You'll be amazed how much it helps. Tuesday was our Lecture Day. We followed each lecture with informal discussion groups, four in number, each led by a program faculty member. The students kept their regular seminar constituencies for these groups, but faculty rotated into them. This way, the students could experience each faculty member occasionally. Wednesday was Chaucer Day. Thursday was Dream Seminar Day. Friday was Faculty Seminar Day.

9) The Book

The book lay at the heart of it all. Part of our original plan (and our NEH proposal) was to write a book with our students on dreams and poetry, and we figured that the research and close work involved in such an endeavor would necessitate a reduced ratio, etc. (We were talking about a published book — one that the students would write, the faculty would edit, and a good publisher would bring out. Our thought was that this would be a great teaching device for an advanced program in the humanities.) So we spent all year working on it. Each student kept a file of his/her writing in the program secretary's office, as did each faculty member. During the summer following the 1973–74 year, the editing was done.

Doing the book was hard. Real hard. Some students used it as something to rebel against. Others loved the idea from start to finish. Some were terrified at the idea of writing for publication. Others couldn't wait to get their names in print. I think it fair to say that the faculty members, if mainly in private, were mercurial on the idea all year long. Sometimes we thought about giving up. And the book's concept kept changing on us. And we were sometimes scared because the students were often so scared. And so on. Four months ago, I told Chuck Pailthorp when we met at the mailbox that I'd never get involved in a goddamned program that had a goddamned *book* in it again.

Now, in retrospect, I think I can see the book pretty clearly. I think that we were fooled because, after all, writing a book seems like an old-fashioned, fairly traditional, thing to do, and we could never understand why it seemed like the strangest thing in the world to be aiming toward. I for one kept thinking: What's going on here? Why is it so hard to do? It should be an almost routine thing for us teachers. What's *wrong?* And the answer is that nothing whatever was wrong. The problem was that none of us had ever written books before except Richard Jones. (Pete and I had written dissertations, but that's different.) And Richard was deciding that he didn't want to write any more books. And the students didn't know any more about writing books than they knew about paleozoic shale.

The important thing is that we didn't give up. Good will and good humor mostly prevailed, and everybody's vacillations on the matter gradually became everybody's soap opera/comedy hour. The book, now entitled *The Dream Poet,* will be brought out by G. K. Hall & Co.

And I have decided to go through the whole thing again this next year in Human Responses to Human Documents.

10) Non-Observance of Quarters.

We didn't pay any attention to the normal three quarters. We took vacations at Christmas and Spring Break like everybody else, but we viewed the program as something that just lasted from October 1st to sometime in June, period. We wrote evaluations at the end (see no. 15).

11) The Research Month.

We picked out the dreariest part of the academic year (weather-wise, which is everything here), February, and turned it into Research Month. During that month, students and faculty worked on their work. Our only scheduled events for that month were our dream seminars, which kept meeting as usual each week. During this month, student-faculty contacts were mainly in the nature of what goes on in individual contracts. This program component was as much for therapy as it was for research. We waited until people were just bone tired of the regular schedule and at the same time totally fed up with the weather (around 10 February or so), and then broke the program up. Most people came back around 10 March feeling a lot better and ready to start up again.

12) Media.

We tape-recorded a lot of seminars. We also videotaped one session for each of the four seminars. (The media folks downstairs managed to lose almost all of our videotaped stuff.) And I think it fair to say that faculty and students alike in this program have had it with videotape. It's just never worth the trouble. And it always is a lot of trouble. My own view on this is a simple one: the videotaping of seminars is a ca. 1965 god that failed. We showed only one film all year. We tried to stay away from machinery of all types as much as we could, while also trying not to bore everybody in earshot with our antitechnological biases and prejudices.

13) At-home Lectures.

We grew tired of the lecture halls and hungry for more social-izing at about the same time. So when we came back from the Research Month a little before the middle of March, we started holding our weekly lectures in the evenings at teachers' and students' homes, in combination with dinner (potluck). We would assemble at the appointed place around 7:00 p.m., and a faculty member would lecture for an hour. (This series of lectures was on poets and poems — one week each for a work by Shakespeare, Arnold, Keats, Blake, Roethke, Coleridge, Wordsworth, and Philip Booth.) The lecture would be followed by discussion and dinner. This idea worked very well, but was hard on the too-regular hostesses, whose home we invaded more than was probably right. I am saying this half-seriously and half-comically, but it is true that this seems to be the only flaw in weekly at-home lectures, and that it should be worked out so that nobody has to be a host or hostess more than once. See Susy Jones for further details.

14) The Faculty Covenant.

We had a two-part faculty covenant. The first part said that conflict resolution among the faculty would be solved by doing whatever the particular faculty member who *felt strongest* about a particular issue wanted to do. The second part said that the faculty was committed to joie de vivre as an overriding principle. Both worked fine and were sufficient.

15) The Evaluation Retreat.

Like other programs, we held an early orientation retreat — ours was at Spirit Lake in October, 1973. But I got one of my infrequent good ideas a little after Spring Break, and came up with the idea of the Evaluation Retreat. So, for the last week of Spring Quarter, 1974, we took a bunch of typewriters, stack upon stack of evaluation forms, and ourselves up to the Fort Worden Conference Center at Port Townsend. At the end of that week, all the conferences had been held and all the evaluations were written. This is the way to do it.

16) *The Year at a Glance.*

The first quarter was a smash. As Pete Sinclair predicted, many of the students picked up Middle English very quickly. Everybody was reading and writing, and everybody was excited about what we were doing. The lectures were great, and seminars were exciting. When we came back from the Christmas holiday, it became evident to the students that we were serious about the book, and they reacted in a variety of ways. (Up to this point, we had lost none of the original students, except through graduation.) So we took the Research Month, returning shortly before mid-March. We went through a period of doldrums, and the faculty had to start counseling. A few students dropped out — all, with the exception of one, in happy circumstances. This was gearshifting time. We were changing the program's focus from learning about dream psychology, Chaucer, poetry, medieval England, aesthetics, etc., into the writing of a book about those things. A lot of people never made it into high, but a lot of people did, and — as I say above — the shift was a success because almost everybody was trying, working, worrying, and at the same time charitable, kind, tolerant, and good humored. The files filled up with writing, and we took off for Fort Worden at the end of May for the Evaluation Retreat. School was over and the book started to be knocked into shape — mainly by Richard Jones. The whole thing went very fast. It seemed successful while we were living it, and it seems successful now.

17) *Conclusion.*

This program was taught by Richard Jones, Tom Maddox, Pete Sinclair, and me. Probably the most important thing to say at this time, and the best way to end this, is that the four of us feel that we'd like to teach the same program again, together, as soon as possible. It was a great program.

Note:

The program faculty spent a good bit of time in counseling the program's graduating seniors and in helping them to realize their various goals for the first year beyond Evergreen. We found that this work paid off really well. Dreams and Poetry graduates are now pursuing graduate studies at The Bank Street College of Education, The Johns Hopkins University, Northwestern University, and other schools. Others have gained positions in counseling and teaching. All I know about are doing really interesting things. My impression is that, contrary to what some people here worry about, our graduates are very much in demand — especially by the country's better graduate schools. But counseling by faculty is important.

Leo Daugherty, Coordinator (Erstwhile)
9 September 1974

6

FINE POINTS

THE RATIO

Because of declining enrollment we have been able to staff some programs at a one to fifteen faculty-student ratio. While bad for the college (for obvious political and economic reasons), this has been good for the experiment. A program can be one hundred percent more effective when this small reduction in ratio can be made. There is a quantum difference between what can happen in a seminar of twelve to fifteen and what can happen in a seminar of seventeen to twenty. And the prospect of writing letters of reflection and transcript evaluations for twenty students can be grim, while for fifteen it can still be a pleasure.

PROGRAM TURF

It is desirable for the faculty to have their offices in close proximity, and for the program to own some lounge or common room space nearby — a place the students can furnish to taste, where messages can be exchanged, where people can meet and small talk. Meiklejohn and Tussman seemed to feel that a whole dormitory or house was necessary; we have found that a common room is sufficient.

PROGRAM TITLES

In-house titles like *Dreams and Poetry* and *Democracy and Tyranny*, while useful for conveying the thematic nature of the programs within the college, are confusing to incoming students and their parents. Subtitles, in traditional academic nomenclature, solve this problem. Thus: *Dreams and Poetry; Advanced Interdisciplinary Studies in Psychology and Literature*, and *Democracy and Tyranny; Basic Interdisciplinary Studies in Western Civilization*. Correspondingly, a student's transcript evaluation should be summarized in the form of a list of suggested course equivalencies in quarter credit hours, in the event the student transfers to a traditional college.

ADVANCED PROGRAMS

Recall that Meiklejohn's and Tussman's were strictly lower division programs. We were able to demonstrate during Evergreen's early years that highly effective programs of coordinated study can be offered at advanced levels; however, we are now learning that advanced programs tend to wither away as an increasing number of juniors and seniors opt for more career-oriented offerings, and as the faculty tries to see that such options exist. A private liberal arts college could probably apply the coordinated studies model across the board. In a state institution, Tussman seems to be right: the place for programs of coordinated study is in the lower division.

THE FIRST MEETING

It is a good idea for each member of the faculty team to introduce himself to the students at the first meeting by way of a brief autobiographical statement – educational background, previous teaching experience, why he chose to join the program. The students are being asked to make an unusual commitment: a year of their college education. They should be given as much information as is possible on which to base last minute reconsiderations.

Each student should also receive a highly detailed program syllabus, which states the program's objectives, and how the faculty has planned to achieve those objectives, and includes a day-by-day schedule of all the activities that have been planned for the first quarter. Students making this radical a change in the pattern of their education need to be reassured that the faculty who planned the program at least appear to know what they are doing. Those who presume that students who are seeking an alternative education are in search of less structure are wrong; what they are in search of is *different* structure. Of course, changes will be made in the program's design and schedule. This is easy when the change called for is from something to something else. The call from nothing to something is not so easy to hear.

Finally, it is important that the coordinator deliver a sermon in which he tries to create visions of the glories and frustrations that lay ahead, as everyone tries to learn how to learn cooperatively; and of the many temptations that will rise up along the way, inviting lapses back into the evils of selfish competition. The sermon will, of course, be forgotten, and its unfamiliar impact will have to be pointed out repeatedly at more strategic moments. But a start has to be made in the conversion process, and the first meeting is not too soon.

SEMINAR ROTATION

There is always the problem of weighing the advantages of multiple exposure – of students to students and students to faculty – against the advantages of program continuity, seminar coherence, and high quality evaluations. Ad hoc solutions seem to be the best. If all of the seminars are happy, and the issue doesn't come up, fine: everyone stays in the same seminars all year and the evaluations are as informed as is possible. If, as is more often the case, one or more of the seminars are having difficulties, a certain amount of tinkering with this or that rotation scheme can be corrective. The one variable which should not be overlooked is evaluation writing. If the exchange of letters of reflection between a student and a faculty member has been productive, every effort should be made to keep the two in the same seminar. At the other end, since the last faculty member to work with a student usually writes the transcript evaluation, every effort should be made to insure that this last contact will be of lengthy duration.

MIDSTREAM TRANSFERS

Inevitably, a few students drop out of a program at the end of the first quarter, and another few drop in from other programs. The drop-outs are no problem; the drop-ins are. One solution has worked particularly well: making the new students' admission into the program contingent on their reading certain key books from the fall quarter book list, and requiring that they attend a make-up workshop on those books in the first month of the winter quarter. This make-up workshop is then led by two of the best veteran students. Two such have always been eager to lead the make-up workshop, have always led it well – and, of course, their own learning is always immeasurably enhanced by the experience. For example, see Crystal Jones' self-evaluation in chapter five.

STUDENT TEACHING

The leading of make-up workshops is not the only teaching activity of which some students have shown themselves to be capable. Currently, there are a dozen or so of my former students leading dream reflection seminars in other programs. Gifted writers can lead writing workshops. Student antiquarians can lead workshops on how to use the library. Students with theatrical experience can organize small performances. A student panel should occasionally take the place of a lecture. And a few select students should occasionally be invited to present a full-blown lecture. (When we first thought of trying this, I feared we might cloud the program's cooperative climate by thus singling out these students. However, their lectures were received with applause and with pats on the back for weeks afterward. Some of our own girls and boys made it, as it were). In any event, the more teaching you can have the students do, the better.

ART, MATHEMATICS AND FOREIGN LANGUAGES

There are still a few diehards on the Evergreen faculty who insist that *anything* can be effectively learned within a well-designed program of coordinated study. I, and I think a majority of colleagues, have come to doubt this. Subjects that do not lend themselves to thematic development in seminars, and subjects that are best learned sequentially, don't fare well in the coordinated studies format. This leaves room for all of the social sciences and the humanities, and for many of the natural sciences. Considering that the format has been used so infrequently in the sixty or so years since Meiklejohn invented it, I think we should not despair if the mathematicians, artists, and linguists have to continue to teach courses.

FACULTY ASSIGNMENT

Programs should be conceived and designed by faculty who are committed to teach in them, and vice versa. Committees can't do the job.

STUDENT INVOLVEMENT IN PROGRAM PLANNING

If the planning is for other students, this is absurd. If the program which the students help to plan is one in which they have preenrolled, their involvement in program planning has been shown by one Evergreen program (Outdoor Education) to have merit. Most of our experience with student involvement in program planning has taken place *within* programs as they evolve over the year. This has usually pertained to such items as scheduling and book choices. It does no harm, and is good for morale.

FILMS

Film versions of many good books are available, and it is nice to be able to enjoy them together as often as the program budget permits. They should be scheduled *after* the book has been read and *after* the seminar.

FESTIVITIES AND SOCIAL ACTIVITIES

Parties, pot lucks, theater trips, and festivals are marvelous additions to a program, and they contribute greatly not only to its general esprit, but to the quality of its academic functions. They should be approved, encouraged, supported and sometimes attended by the faculty, but they should always be planned and organized by the students. Students are better at these things, and they have the time for them.

THE NOVEMBER SLUMP

Around Thanksgiving (although it has been known to come as late as February) a certain amount of serious grumbling occurs in the ranks. Too much work, the books are too hard, not enough time, we don't understand the theme, we'll never get it done, things aren't fitting together, we need more lectures, etc. The students may call a special meeting to air these complaints. This is a good sign. It means that the integrative nature of the program's objectives is beginning to register, and that the students are feeling the difference between working in a program and taking courses. The faculty should respond to these complaints. They may use a faculty seminar to compose a position paper on the current status of the program in respect to the theme or project, distribute the paper and hold an extra all-program meeting to discuss it. They may join with the students in a special meeting as a panel. Reasonable requests (minor schedule changes, an extra lecture or two) may be acceded to. Flaws in the fine tuning of the design should be admitted and corrected. Most importantly, however, the faculty should stand firm in support of the program's basic organization, and in support of the original objectives. All meetings addressed to the complaints should be extra ones, and not be allowed to displace regularly scheduled activities. The complaints should be taken seriously, in other words, but should be seen for what they are: intellectual growing pains. The crisis (if it comes to that) is an opportunity for the faculty to reaffirm its faith in the program and in the students. They'll receive compliments for doing so, come spring. In programs which fail, it is the faculty, not the program, about which the students complain, and, in that event, they are more likely to express complaints with their feet than with their mouths.

CONTINUITY AND PREDICTABILITY

The Evergreen planning faculty's biggest mistake was to proscribe the repeating of programs. Given the state of the art, the casual assumption that successful programs would come easily was a foolish one. Many of Evergreen's successful programs, which should have been repeated (with, perhaps, some changes in faculty team composition) have not been, because of that early cavalier decision. It has been the primary cause of the college's underenrollment. Who wants to enroll in a college in which no one knows what will be taught the year after next, and in which it is impossible to follow your friend's, or older sister's, suggestion of program choice? The college is now trying to correct that early mistake by offering and advertising previously successful programs. However this may turn out, put it down as a guiding principle that a successful program of coordinated study should be repeated, at least in some variation. The relearning that is required of a faculty team in order to make a program succeed is too valuable to waste. Half of the anxiety of teaching in a program is watching to see if the design is working. When it has worked, at least some of the faculty team deserve the luxury of teaching it, knowing that it works.

7

PROSPECTUS

An accident of history took an educational experiment which began (and quickly ended) on the peripheries of two venerable universities, and made it the focal mission of an upstart alternative state college. A more radical variation in the conditions of an experiment would be hard to think of. The Wisconsin experiment was premature. The Berkeley experiment was so limited that it could only be tentatively described. The Evergreen experiment has had a comparatively long life and has been so broadly applied that I had to be extremely selective in documenting my report of it.

Overshadowing all else that the experiment at Evergreen has added to the knowledge gained from the experiments at Wisconsin and Berkeley is the discovery that when results are positive they are exceedingly so, and that when they are negative they are awful. The collaborative teaching model seems to be endogenously immune to mediocrity. It succeeds or it fails; it yields extraordinary satisfaction or it enervates. In either case, the experience is *shared*.

Both the Berkeley and the Evergreen experiments showed the key variable to be that of staffing. Tussman couldn't recruit sufficient faculty at Berkeley to sustain the experiment. At

Evergreen, we committed so many faculty to the experiment that controlling it has been a problem. These, I believe, are the findings which should inform speculations on what may lie ahead in the story of Meiklejohn's invention.

The possibility of discriminate staffing should be the first consideration of any institution that wishes to try its hand at offering programs of coordinated study. Ideally, the faculty team should consist of professors who are experienced teachers of courses, who are themselves in search of an alternative and who *choose* to place at least a year of their professional lives on the same line.

Even at Evergreen the collaborative teaching model is now being used more selectively. But Evergreen's primary role in the story has almost been played out. This role had to have been a transitional one, since not many new colleges are going to be built in America's foreseeable future, much less ones which proscribe requirements, grades, majors, departments, courses, faculty rank and tenure. Evergreen had to eschew these traditional features of college life in order to test the potentials of collaborative interdisciplinary teaching to their possible limits. We have been like the greenhouse phase of an agricultural experiment: the plant has been shown to thrive under a sufficient number of special conditions to deserve its natural evolution in the field. If collaborative interdisciplinary education is to have a future, traditional systems of higher education will have to find ways to assimilate it. The actual shape that this future may assume will depend on conditioning factors that are unlikely to develop at The Evergreen State College for a variety of local reasons.

Many American colleges are presently having difficulty adjusting to the transition from the seller's market, to which they had grown accustomed, to the buyer's market into which the ending of the Vietnam war surprised them. Retrenchments and reductions in force are no longer uncommon. In these circumstances, the boards of trustees of some underenrolled traditional colleges may come to view the prospect of encouraging experimentation with collaborative teaching as a promising way to heighten institutional visibility.*

---

*From the beginning, Evergreen's student population has included an extraordinarily high percentage of nonresidents. Twenty-five percent

The condition that is more likely to invite further experimentation with the collaborative teaching model is, however, one that prevailed before the national college enrollment fall-off: *teaching in a traditional college tends to be boring.* For many professors the redeeming feature of the job is that it yields full-time pay for part-time work. There are other ways, of course, to make the job satisfying, and many professors genuinely enjoy the scholarly activities which they engage while not having to teach — and work hard at them. (The many who don't still enjoy the time off from teaching that academic tradition has arranged for those who do.) The exceptions aside, it is well known, if not widely admitted, that many college professors are bored with what they do as teachers. Not a few faculties, who do no publishing that is worth mentioning, have nonetheless made the avoidance of teaching a publicly supported point of professional pride.

Much of this boredom stems, I think, not from the characters of the college professors, but from the conditions of their work, made inevitable by college teaching having become synonymous with having to teach courses. Having to teach courses contains the very ingredients of boredom: it is lonely, isolated, and repetitive. You can seldom be sure that what you are doing as a teacher has any effects on whatever learning may be going on in the students, and, if so, what kinds of effects those are. The typical conclusion reached over the years

---

is the figure usually referred to, but this is a base minimum figure, since it includes only those students who are actually paying nonresident tuition. Washington law allows nonresidents to apply for resident status after one year, so that many students who are currently enrolled as residents of Washington originally came to the College from other states. Students have been attracted to Evergreen from every state in the union and from 26 other nations. In the fall of 1977, 116 students came from California, 47 from Illinois, 33 from Massachusetts, 22 from Minnesota, 23 from New Jersey, 50 from New York, 42 from Ohio, and 65 from Oregon. All of this national recruiting is sustained by a student grapevine; Washington law prohibits using state funds to recruit nonresidents.

Every year since 1974, more students have enrolled from California than have enrolled from the College's home county. As a state college, charged with serving the educational needs of Southwest Washington, this enrollment pattern has been an embarrassment. In a similar situation, a private college, able to fund a modest national recruitment campaign, would obviously have a long waiting list.

is that, since only a few of the students make an impression in any given course, it must be the students who make the difference and not the teaching. The only thing that seems to change, from year to year, are the students, and, after a while, even they tend to congeal into "types."

And it is so very easy to cheat yourself: to hide from your mistakes and to pretend to be someone, or something, you know you are not. The occasional artist finds ways of circumventing these conditions, but many a college professor succumbs to them by coming to agree that the teaching is – indeed – a "load" and by going on to take solace in the fact that only nine to twelve hours a week of it has to be done.

A significant number of college professors might opt to change these working conditions by following the coordinated study model, if they knew of it – which is the purpose of publishing this report.

It is impossible for the teaching that goes on in a program of coordinated study to be boring. When it isn't satisfying, it can be frightening, frustrating, or embarrassing – but it is impossible for it to be boring. To an experienced teacher of courses, it doesn't even feel like teaching. It cannot be lonely, isolated, or repetitive. And, since you are totally responsible for the educations of a knowable number of students, for a whole academic year, vivid knowledge of the effects of what you are doing as a teacher cannot fail to accrue. Every student makes a distinct impression.

And opportunities for kidding yourself are almost nil. You almost never get to coast, or rest on a reputation. Almost every feeling of accomplishment has to be earned. Almost every sense of recognition must come from having kept your promises. Teaching, as a member of the faculty team in a program of coordinated study, is, in other words, good for your character.

Most college professors are extraordinarily intelligent men and women who have chosen to live modest lives, in order to live interesting ones. Having to teach, by way of having to teach courses, cuts many of them off from what attracted them to the profession in the first place: being responsible for the cultivation of learning. In a program of coordinated study, there is no danger of ever losing this sense of responsibility. This is the exit from boredom that the Evergreen replication of the Berkeley and Wisconsin experiments has shown to be possible: to renew the view of what it can mean to teach in college, by committing yourself to total responsibility for it, in the professional intimacy of colleagues who are on the same watch. With far less experience than many of my colleagues and I have had, Tussman was able to say this of it:

> A group of students and faculty set out, in the midst of a powerful, ongoing, somewhat turbulent institution, to develop and engage in a radically different mode of educational life. We were doing not only what we had not been doing before but what others around us were not doing. And we were a more or less conventional group of faculty members and a fairly representative group of Berkeley freshmen.

> We quickly came to realize how much shelter the normal classroom situation provides for the professor. He sees his class TuTh or MWF for an hour. Students arrive, pause briefly, and depart. The professor is clearly in charge. He is on his own ground, a plenary grade wielder, protected by tradition and "academic freedom" from external and even colleagial scrutiny. He is responsible for only a small fraction of the students' education and need not concern himself about what happens elsewhere or about what it all adds up to. He faces a collection of individuals who are generally strangers to each other and who have only the slightest transient identity as a "group." Only extremely good or extremely bad teaching can transform a class into a community capable of developing and asserting the power of its own peer-group culture. And the subject, defined in disciplinary terms, permits the formulation of issues or problems in ways appropriate to the special perspective of the discipline and the professor. The standard mood is academic.

> In our program, however, the faculty was without its usual insulation. We were exposed to each other at the point of the exercise of the art of teaching. And we were in contact with students in

a radically different way. We were aware that we were almost entirely responsible for the students' education. The core problems — war and peace, freedom and authority, order and chaos — were problems with which they were vitally concerned, and the stakes were not merely academic tokens and counters. Moreover, the students came to know each other and to develop something of a sense of themselves as a group with interests which called for expression and assertion. (*Experiment at Berkeley*, pp. 92-93.)

The departmentalization which defines the mores of traditional college life will give some logistical resistance to collaborative teaching, but this may prove to be healthy resistance. Younger faculty will not want to (and should not) jeopardize their careers by taking lengthy leaves from departmental responsibilities. (Actually, from the point of view of their eventually doing well in the coordinated study mode, younger faculty should be learning how to teach good courses, anyway.) It is *tenured* faculty (usually, the most bored with their teaching) who have nothing to lose by taking leaves from departmental responsibilities, in order to refresh the impulses which led them to tenure in the first place. Given administrative sanction, they have only to locate kindred spirits among colleagues in other departments, dream up an interesting program design, secure the cooperation of the office of the registrar, do some student recruiting and proceed to live a year of mutual unsettlement together. Thus, the department structure may ultimately serve to assure that the programs of coordinated study that do get tried in traditional colleges will meet the criterion for success which both the Berkeley and Evergreen experiments have shown to be the penultimate criterion: discriminate staffing. (I have even permitted myself the fantasy that on some campus, someday, the license to begin teaching in programs of coordinated study will be regarded as one of the privileges that tenure bestows).

The most resistance to the assimilation process will stem from the fact that teaching in programs of coordinated study increases the faculty's working hours. Some evenings and weekends have to be given over to reading good books that one would otherwise not feel called upon to read. Writing must sometimes be done, for the lectures and the faculty seminars, which there is no time to think of publishing. Evaluation will take the thirty hours needed to compose letters, rather than the two that it takes to get the grades done. And preparation for each seminar may be accompanied by anticipations of testing integrity instead of by temptations to show off.

The question, then, that the Meiklejohn–Tussman–Cadwallader–Evergreen collaborative teaching model may come to pose to some college professors is, at the bottom line: Is it worthwhile to work more at something that is interesting than it is to work less at something that is boring?

That's the personal question. The cultural one is why some of the alternative colleges mentioned in the preface to this report have had to forfeit their experimental mandates, while The Evergreen State College has, for the most part, been able to maintain the integrity of its conception for ten years? I think the answer is that the experiment at Evergreen became not only a reaction to the problematic sixties, but an *action* which was organically rooted in an articulate and instructive past. As such, the experiment at Evergreen may inform the *promises* which may be made by some future colleges to some future generations, as Meiklejohn's and Tussman's experiments informed Evergreen's promises.*

Meiklejohn's report of the experiment at Wisconsin is tedious. It goes on and on in the voice of a disinterested philosopher of the 1920s, who would rather be engaged in debating politely than in writing an account of an experiment that was about to be stopped. The report does come to a point, however, and that point may be where the personally and culturally based motives of some college professors and some colleges may someday meet. In summing up his recommendations to the University of Wisconsin's College of Letters

---

*I use the words *action* and *promises* as Hannah Arendt defines them in *The Human Condition* (University of Chicago Press, 1958.)

and Science, and to an unknown American future, in 1931, Meiklejohn had this to say:

> Probably the most profound impression which has been made upon the faculty by their adventure in the teaching of young Americans has been the sense of their own lack of adequate liberal education. . . .
>
> We do not teach liberal understanding well chiefly because we do not know what it is. We are very much at home in the field of scholarship. If a student will limit his interest to some field of intellectual abstraction, we can show him what the human mind has thus far done in that field. . . .
>
> But if the liberal question is asked, our skill and mastery vanish. . . .
>
> How can it be brought about that the teachers in our colleges and universities shall see themselves, not only as the servants of scholarship, but also, in a far deeper sense, as the creators of the national intelligence. . . . Intelligence, wisdom, sensitiveness, generosity — these cannot be set aside from our planning, to be, as it were, by-products of the scholarly pursuits. . . .
>
> If, then, one is set to inquire how American teaching can be better done, the most fundamental phases of the inquiry must concern themselves with the forces which create and fashion the attitude, the life, of the American teacher. (*The Experimental College,* pp. 315-318.)

That was written in 1931, when it was possible to appeal to sentiments of national altruism without anticipating second looks. Today, such talk makes us feel squeamish. And so I find myself concluding this report, in 1980, by appealing to the *personal* interests of college professors, and against the *personal* boredom of their jobs (refraining from making it a point of emphasis that a personal venture may also be a moral one).

In any event, the major implication raised by the experiment at Evergreen is that the protean conditions of faculty work life, which Meiklejohn and Tussman described as *incidental* to the artful teaching of a *particular* liberal curriculum, may be prescriptive in the artful teaching of *any* liberal curriculum. If we define a liberal curriculum, as Meiklejohn did in 1920, as one in which the instruction is dominated by no special interest, but is intended to take human activity as a whole, to understand human endeavors not in their isolation but in their relations to one another, it is easy to see why Leo Daugherty could say in his introduction to this report: ". . . the liberal arts — an awful lot of lip-service to the contrary — are decidedly not where the action is." For, leaving aside the growing cultural demands for preprofessional, paraprofessional, and vocational education which Daugherty cited, it may be that trying to offer a liberal arts curriculum by way of separate teachers, teaching separate courses, to separate groups of students is a contradiction within itself. It would be a rare teacher who, in modern times, could achieve the breadth of knowledge necessary to teach such a curriculum within the ambience of a single course. And it would be an exceedingly improbable set of coincidences which would permit a series of uncoordinated courses to constitute such a curriculum.

I have not made a study of the so-called liberal arts colleges in America which have sought to meet Meiklejohn's criteria, and have failed. Nor have I the opportunity and will to do so. However, my experience in the Evergreen experiment — and in the writing of this report — prompt me to venture a diagnosis of the many such failures which have surely occurred: They were not the result of faulty conceptual planning, nor of lack of imagination in their construction. They failed *in their execution* (or, if you will, in their "delivery") and this failure was made inevitable by the isolated — and isolating — teaching conditions which are made necessary by defining teaching as teaching courses. This diagnosis has been most strongly suggested by vivid personal memories of having taught at Evergreen in programs of coordinated study whose original conceptions and constructions proved in retrospect to have been less than excellent, but whose actual provisions of a truly liberal education were dramatically effective. I am now convinced that it is not enough to *intend* "to take human activity as a whole, to understand human endeavors not in their isolation but in their relations to one another. . . ." The conditions of one's work as a teacher must be conducive to the realization of those intentions. A curriculum which consists of separately taught courses is not conducive to this — however fondly its planners may have hoped that its constituent pieces might somehow find felicitously liberating arrangements in the various efforts of the students to put them together. On the other hand, it has been shown that a curriculum whose *structural* features require collaborative interdisciplinary teaching is highly conducive to the realization of liberal intentions — even when the original intentions are subsequently shown to have been less than optimally liberal.

What are those structural features? I repeat:

1. A small faculty team drawn from different disciplines.

2. Working together full-time for a full year.

3. With a reasonable number of students who are also working together full-time.

4. With the aim of representing, not teaching, their subjects.

5. In the common exploration of a theme or problem (or completion of a project) which no single discipline can articulate.

6. With weekly opportunities, in faculty seminars, to enjoy an understanding of their several disciplines, not in their isolation but in their relations to one another.

Meiklejohn seems to have anticipated all of this when he concluded his report as follows:

> The primary question concerning our academic system is not "What is its effect upon the students?" but rather, "What is its effect upon our teachers?" If we can get them rightly placed in relation to their work, nothing in the world can prevail against them." (*The Experimental College,* p. 318.)

Our experience at Evergreen does not support Meiklejohn's final burst of optimism there, but it does support his distinguishment of the primary question concerning our academic system: *What are its effects on our teachers?* As an all too general beginning of an answer to this question, the experiment at Evergreen confirms Meiklejohn's prescience when he said:

> What we need to consider is not an addition to our teaching procedure, but a transformation of it. (*The Experimental College*, p. 266.)